PERSONAL FINANCIAL FITNESS: SECOND EDITION

How To Improve The Health Of Your Wealth

Allen Klosowski, CFP

CRISP PUBLICATIONS, INC.
Los Altos, California

PERSONAL FINANCIAL FITNESS: SECOND EDITION

How To Improve The Health Of Your Wealth

Allen Klosowski, CFP

CREDITS
Editor: **Michael G. Crisp**
Designer: **Carol Harris**
Typesetting: **Interface Studio**
Cover Design: **Carol Harris**
Artwork: **Ralph Mapson**

Copyright © 1989 by Crisp Publications, Inc.
Printed in the United States of America

English language Crisp books are distributed worldwide. Our major international distributors include:

CANADA: Reid Publishing, LTD., Box 7267, Oakville, Ontario Canada L6J 6L6. TEL: (416) 842-4428, FAX: (416) 842-9327

AUSTRALIA: Career Builders, P. O. Box 1051, Springwood, Brisbane, Queensland, Australia 4127. TEL: 841-1061, FAX: 841-1580

NEW ZEALAND: Career Builders, P. O. Box 571, Manurewa, Auckland, New Zealand. TEL: 266-5276, FAX: 266-4152

JAPAN: Phoenix Associates Co., Mizuho Bldg. 2-12-2, Kami Osaki, Shinagawa-Ku, Tokyo 141, Japan. TEL: 443-7231, FAX: 443-7640

Selected Crisp titles are also available in other languages. Contact International Rights Manager Tim Polk at (415) 949-4888 for more information.

Library of Congress Catalog Card Number 86-71571
Klosowski, Allen
Personal Financial Fitness
ISBN 0-931961-89-0

TO THE READER

Regular exercise, good nutrition and a positive mental outlook can greatly improve the quality of your life. So can financial planning. The benefits derived will vary with the amount of time and effort you invest. It is never too early to initiate financial planning—nor is it ever too late. The most important thing is to **get started.** This program has been designed to help you do just that.

Financial planning should be at the heart of your life's planning. Only with a sound financial basis will you be free to enjoy and appreciate all of the other aspects of life—social, educational, recreational, family, and retirement.

This book will help you become financially fit and will provide a practical hands on approach to not only determine where you are now, but also provide specific information about how to achieve the level of financial security you desire. How you apply the advice in this book depends on how important money and the things it provides are to you.

To receive the most benefit from this book, all activities and exercises should be completed. It is then recommended you review any material that you desire more information on with a person who has financial expertise. This will insure you have understood the information and concepts presented and are applying them correctly. Good luck!

Allen Klosowski, CFP

ABOUT THE AUTHOR

Allen Klosowski, CFP—is a Certified Financial Planner and member of the Registry of Financial Planning Practitioners. Mr. Klosowski is a Registered Investment Advisor who has advised clients on financial matters since 1969. He regularly conducts seminars for corporations, hospital foundations, and charitable organizations.

If you wish to contact Mr. Klosowski regarding your financial situation, you may either write or call:

Allen Klosowski, CFP
Jeanco Financial, Inc.
2082 Business Center Drive, Suite 165
Irvine, California 92715

Telephone: 1 (714) 752-1396

ACKNOWLEDGMENTS

I wish to thank my associate, Ann Woodson, CFP, for her many ideas and suggestions throughout the development of the manuscript. Her continual support made this book possible.

A special thanks to my parents who have been a constant source of encouragement and inspiration to me.

PREFACE TO THE FIRST EDITION

The purpose of this book is twofold. It will:

1. Add to your knowledge and understanding of money management so you can invest your funds more effectively.

2. Expand your thinking so that any financial advice or recommendation you receive will be more understandable. In essence, this book should help you gain a new perspective on personal financial planning.

A fitness program will be prescribed. However, instead of calisthentics, you'll be "working out" with a pencil. With practice, the financial fitness program will eventually become a part of your day-to-day living, much like a regular exercise program or proper eating habits.

If diligently followed, the financial fitness program should enable you to *reduce* taxes, *increase* investment income, *build* wealth faster, and lay a solid foundation for major events such as the education of your children or your retirement.

PREFACE TO THE SECOND EDITION

During the two years since the first edition appeared, several changes (some more subtle than others), have encouraged an updated revision to *Personal Financial Fitness.* Thanks to the input from readers and reviewers, we have taken a successful, highly regarded book and have done our best to make it better.

Particular attention has been paid to the insurance section and the investment section, where much new information has been added. Other, more modest changes have been made throughout to insure the book reflects the most current information on sound financial planning.

We will make every effort to maintain the quality and up-to-date information in subsequent editions.

CONTENTS

SECTION I

FINANCIAL PLANNING

An Overview

WHAT IS PERSONAL FINANCIAL PLANNING?

Personal financial planning is nothing more than the development and implementation of a *comprehensive* plan to help a person achieve some specific financial goals. The idea is to focus on these goals as the starting point in a financial planning process rather than simply use one or more financial instruments (investments) to solve financial problems.

In the planning process, an individual's financial affairs (i.e., investments, savings programs, insurance, retirement plans, estate plan, and so forth) should be considered as a coordinated whole, rather than on a piecemeal basis. This means that financial considerations such as stocks, bonds, life insurance, real estate holdings, and estate planning techniques should be considered in terms of a person's overall financial goals rather than in isolation. Most financially secure people use a variety of financial instruments to achieve their goals and objectives.

Lawyers, accountants, bankers, trust officers, investment advisors, insurance agents, stock brokers, tax specialists, and financial planners can all help an individual to meet his or her specific financial objectives. In fact, most people need to deal with several professionals (practitioners) to receive the quality of expert advice that is needed for the most effective financial planning. This makes coordinating the advice among these experts very important.

Coordination of financial advice might be termed a "systems approach" toward meeting financial goals. Financial planning integrates the basic principles of each specialist into a cohesive approach for each individual. This kind of systems approach is increasingly evident in personal financial planning. In effect, a financial planner, in concert with other professionals, acts as the lead doctor to diagnose and treat those with financial ailments.

Financial planning can help answer many "what if's" in life such as:

- What if I want to purchase a more expensive home?

- What if I decide to go into business for myself?

- What if my children go to college?

- What if my spouse stops working?

- What if I decide to retire at age 55 instead of age 65?

Financial planning is dynamic. It involves taking action and includes decision-making such as whether to move, buy a car, find a new job, etc. These decisions will initiate various actions, each with its own consequences. Both the financial decisions and consequences must be evaluated in an objective manner. Your personal commitment is essential. The time you invest in planning now will pay dividends later.

THE PLANNING PROCESS IS ACTION AND RESULTS ORIENTED

A GREATER NEED FOR FINANCIAL PLANNING

In today's increasingly complex world, everyone needs some financial planning. A bewildering array of investment opportunities, economic swings, and constantly changing tax laws, leads to confusion and frustration. Also, many people have some financial goals they wish to attain, but often these goals are vaguely defined.

Economic ups and downs in the United States, combined with changes in the tax laws, has increased the need for (and complexity of) financial planning. Our affluent society has increased the number of people who need tax, investment, insurance, retirement, and estate planning. These services are readily available, but the extent of services needed vary for each individual.

Central to the planning process is the development of personal financial goal setting. Unfortunately, most people (even those with goals) do not follow consistent policies when making financial decisions. Instead, they react to day-to-day problems or advertising claims. Those with a financial plan are in a position to make more rational financial decisions.

A CRITICAL DECISION: DO I NEED THE SERVICES OF A FINANCIAL PLANNER?

COMPLETE THIS BRIEF SELF ANALYSIS

	YES	NO
• Can I be objective in assessing my personal circumstances?	⎯⎯	⎯⎯
• Do I have time to keep track of my investments?	⎯⎯	⎯⎯
• Do I possess the knowledge of investments, taxation and changes in the law to make intelligent decisions?	⎯⎯	⎯⎯
• Can I avoid procrastinating when decisive action must be taken?	⎯⎯	⎯⎯

If you *cannot* answer yes to the questions listed above, you should consider the services of a financial planner. Please complete all of the exercises in this book before making a decision. More information on services offered by financial planners and whether you should use one will be provided later in this book beginning on page 113.

THE FINANCIAL PLANNING PROCESS

Like a holistic approach to personal health, the process of providing financial fitness involves four basic steps. If you have the time, objectivity and expertise in investments, taxation, insurance, and estate planning, you can complete this four step process on your own. However, most people find it helpful to seek the aid of various professionals to derive the most benefit from this comprehensive process.

Let's review the four step action process:

1. **Examine:** It is important to first develop a profile of your financial health. This is accomplished by gathering and organizing your financial and personal data.

   Your financial data should include a current tax return; a listing of your assets and liabilities; a breakdown of your monthly living expenses; information about your personal and company retirement plans; life, health, and casualty insurance policies you own plus any estate plan documents (wills or trusts) that you have.

   Your personal data should include information on all family members; a clarification of your goals and objectives and an accurate assessment about your tolerance for risk.

2. **Diagnose:** This step should analyze the data that has been gathered to determine your strengths and weaknesses. Proven concepts and principles may then be applied to reach decisions regarding aspects of your financial situation.

   For example, your cash reserves should be reviewed. Are they sufficient? Are they equal to at least three months fixed living expenses? Are you hindered by too much debt? Are your current (liquid) assets sufficient to meet all current obligations (those due within the next twelve month period)?

   Also, do your investments match your stated goals and objectives? If income is your goal, would you consider a certificate of deposit or a money market account more appropriate than a portfolio of speculative stock issues?

3. **Prescribe:** This step is where specific courses of financial action are selected.

For example, if one of your objectives is to generate tax free income, you (or your financial planner) might select an investment in a municipal bond fund. If you desired greater growth potential for a portion of your cash reserves, mutual funds or stocks might be more appropriate.

A desire to provide for your survivors in the event of your death would call for the drafting of an estate plan to meet your specific requests.

4. **Monitor:** You and/or your planner need to review your plan on a regular basis (at least annually) to make appropriate adjustments based upon changes in economic, financial and/or your personal circumstances.

This regular "follow-up" will also provide an opportunity to compare results with your goals and objectives.

Most of your time and effort will be spent in Step 1 and Step 2 of the financial planning process. Gathering personal and financial data and then evaluating your strengths, weaknesses, and needs is the foundation of solid financial planning.

SECTION II

EXAMINE AND DIAGNOSE

How To Determine Your Current Financial Condition

There are several exercises in this section designed to determine your overall financial condition. First, your financial pulse will be taken. Then, you will be asked to gather financial data regarding your income, expenditures, and your present net worth. The section will conclude with information about the types of insurance plans you have in force.

> ## "YOU ARE WHAT YOU THINK."
>
> ## "THINK AND GROW RICH."
>
> ## "KNOW WHAT YOU WANT AND YOU WILL GENERALLY GET IT."

These sayings emphasize the importance of attitude in life. Attitude is simply the way you view things—mentally and emotionally. If you are positive and progressive in your outlook, you almost certainly will get more out of life than if you are negative and defensive.

How you view financial matters generally, and money specifically, will greatly influence your financial success. To begin, take your financial pulse using the exercise on the facing page. It will help inform you about your attitude and awareness of your current financial situation.

TAKING YOUR FINANCIAL PULSE

	Yes	No	I Don't Know
Do you have well defined personal financial goals?	____	____	____
Do you view your financial future with enthusiasm and confidence?	____	____	____
Do you know what you are worth?	____	____	____
Do you save money on a regular basis?	____	____	____
Are you currently receiving any tax-free income?	____	____	____
Do you have any investments that help to reduce your taxable income?	____	____	____
Do you qualify for a deductible IRA contribution?	____	____	____
Do you take advantage of all company sponsored savings/investment programs?	____	____	____
Do you feel you have sufficient permanent life insurance coverage?	____	____	____
Do you feel your estate plan (will/trust) accomplishes your family objectives?	____	____	____
Does an accountant prepare your tax return?	____	____	____
Do you use the services of a professional financial planner?	____	____	____
Can you distinguish between spending and saving?	____	____	____
Do you diversify your investments?	____	____	____
Do you take full responsibility for your financial affairs?	____	____	____
Do you spend less than you earn?	____	____	____
Do you have a plan to retire in comfort?	____	____	____
Do you avoid major credit card purchases?	____	____	____
Have you planned for your children's college education?	____	____	____
Are you generally satisfied with your investments?	____	____	____

Total number marked No or I Don't Know	11-20	Weak pulse. The fitness program in this book should help.
	5-10	On the right track, but you need to improve.
	0- 4	You are in good shape. Keep up the good work.

THINK AND GROW RICH
(THE POWER OF POSITIVE THINKING)

Personal financial planning is a process designed to help you accomplish your goals. The nature of your goals and the way they are met is of critical importance in your planning process. Financial goals are never static. What may be appropriate or desirable at one point in your life may not be so a few months later. The process of financial planning is on-going. To begin, ask yourself these questions:

---

1. Where am I now financially?

2. Where do I want to be in the future?

3. How am I going to get there?

Keep the above three questions in mind as you begin your goal setting.

GOAL SETTING PROCESS

1. Be specific—   *Set target dates*

2. Quantify your goals—   *Use numbers*

3. Visualize your goals—   *Picture yourself having already attained your goal, to strengthen your resolve to succeed.*

Example:

POOR: I want to live comfortably when I retire.

BETTER: I want to retire in 10 years (at age 62), and live in a condominium in Phoenix, Arizona with a net monthly income of $2,000.

By wording each of your goals in this manner, progress can be measured on a regular (i.e., annual) basis.

Now that you have an idea of how to properly formulate financial goals, take time to complete the exercise on the facing page regarding your personal goals.

GOAL SETTING—DO IT NOW!

Goal setting is like taking a trip. To be successful, you must know where you are going before you can get there.

Take a moment to list your most important financial goals:

Short term—(two years or less)
(Example: pay-off auto loan in 18 months)

- _____

  _____

- _____

  _____

- _____

  _____

Long term—(in excess of two years)
(Example: retire in 10 years at age 55 to Florida and own a $100,000 home)

- _____

  _____

- _____

  _____

- _____

  _____

Once you have listed some key goals, next list some specific items that may help or hinder the attainment of these goals.

List three (action) items that will help you achieve the short and long term goals you listed on the previous page.
(Example: start a monthly savings plan.)

- _____

- _____

- _____

List three obstacles that may impede the attainment of the short and long term goals you listed.
(Example: excessive monthly credit card balances)

- _____

- _____

- _____

Goal setting is important because:

1. It makes you (and your family) examine your values and clarify them in writing.

2. It enables you to plan ways to use available resources to reach your goals.

3. It puts you in charge and enables you to take control of your money and your life.

IF IT ISN'T WRITTEN, IT ISN'T A GOAL!

THREE IMPORTANT FINANCIAL STATEMENTS

Now that your most important financial goals have been defined and you have a basic idea of what it will take to accomplish them, the following three financial exercises will help you determine your overall financial condition:

1. Completion of an **Income Statement**. The income statement is simply a listing of all of your **income** and **expenses**. It enables you to see what you need to live on and how much you can allocate to savings and investments in order to accomplish your goals.

    Recording and tracking your spending habits will help you formulate judgments about what is most important to you and when to shift your priorities.

2. Completion of a **Balance Sheet**. This is an inventory of your financial resources. It shows what you have to work with as a starting point in the planning process.

3. Developing a **Budget**. This is a projection of **future** expenditures. It will help you control consumption (day-to-day living expenses) and teach you to save money.

Once you have completed a personal income statement, balance sheet and budget, you should review the goals you recorded on page 15 to determine if they can be accomplished with your current financial resources.

Completing these three financial exercises also has some additional benefits. The information you gather can serve as an aid in filling out credit applications, settling an estate and/or preparing your income tax return.

PERSONAL INCOME STATEMENT

The Income Statement is actually an income *and* expense statement. It summarizes where your income for a given period of time (monthly, quarterly, or annually) comes from, and how it was spent.

The Income Statement can, therefore, determine whether you are in control of your finances (showing a surplus) or if you are experiencing a cash flow crisis (showing a deficit).

On the facing page, list all of your various sources of income and expenses for a given period of time (for example, on an annual basis). For some items it will be necessary to compute an average figure based upon past records.

A completed sample Income Statement for the Charles and Barbara Thomas family can be studied on pages 20-22. It would be a good idea to review this information before beginning work on your Income Statement.

INCOME (OR CASH FLOW) STATEMENT

FOR THE PERIOD BEGINNING _____
AND ENDING _____

EARNED INCOME (Before Taxes)

Salary and Wages
   Husband   _____
   Wife   _____
Bonus   _____
Self-Employment Income   _____
Annuities or Pensions   _____
Social Security Payments   _____
Alimony/Child Support   _____
• Other   _____
• Other   _____

INVESTMENT INCOME

Interest   _____
Dividends   _____
Rental Income   _____
• Other   _____
• Other   _____

                          INCOME (A) $ _____

FIXED EXPENSES

Housing—Rent/Mortgage   _____
Utilities   _____
Loan Payments   _____
Taxes
  • Federal and State   _____
  • Social Security   _____
  • Property   _____
Insurance Premiums   _____
• Other   _____
• Other   _____

              FIXED EXPENSES (B) $ _____

VARIABLE EXPENSES

Food   _____
Clothing   _____
Travel/Recreation   _____
Household Maintenance   _____
Transportation   _____
Education   _____
Medical Expenses   _____
Church and Charity   _____
Spending Money   _____
• Other   _____
• Other   _____

          VARIABLE EXPENSES (C) $ _____

TOTAL INCOME (A) $ _____
LESS TOTAL EXPENSES (B + C) $ _____
SURPLUS/(DEFICIT) $ _____

(SAMPLE)
INCOME (OR CASH FLOW) STATEMENT

Charles and Barbara Thomas
FOR THE PERIOD BEGINNING 1-1-XX
AND ENDING 12-31-XX

EARNED INCOME (Before Taxes)

Salary and Wages	
Husband	36,000
Wife	18,000
Bonus	
Self Employment Income	
Annuities or Pensions	
Social Security Payments	
Alimony/Child Support	
• Other	

INVESTMENT INCOME

Interest	720
Dividends	100
Rental Income	
• Other	

INCOME (A) $ 54,820

FIXED EXPENSES

Housing—Rent/Mortgage	3,600
Utilities	760
Loan Payments	900
Taxes	
• Federal and State	8,713
• Social Security	3,861
• Property	650
Insurance Premiums	3,300
• Other	2,400

FIXED EXPENSES (B) $ 24,184

VARIABLE EXPENSES

Food	5,200
Clothing	3,000
Travel/Recreation	3,100
Household Maintenance	800
Transportation	1,250
Education	
Medical Expenses	250
Church and Charity	800
Spending Money	2,400
• Other	

VARIABLE EXPENSES (C) $ 16,800

TOTAL INCOME (A)	$ 54,820
LESS TOTAL EXPENSES (B + C)	$ 40,984
SURPLUS/(DEFICIT)	$ 13,836

INSTRUCTIONS TO THE SAMPLE INCOME STATEMENT

In the example on page 20, we are using a one year period—January-December. You may use a shorter period of time, if you desire, such as a quarter of a year or a month, but an income statement for a year is a good place to start.

Have your checkbook handy. It will be of immeasurable help when you determine your expenses for a given period of time.

INCOME

Salary, wages, and bonuses—list gross amount earned.

Self-employment income—if you have your own business, list the gross income earned.

Annuities, pensions—money from company retirement plans.

Social Security—list payments for you (and your spouse, if applicable).

Alimony/Child Support—enter total amounts received.

INVESTMENT INCOME

Interest—money received from money market accounts, savings accounts, certificates of deposit, bonds, etc.

Dividends—income received from individual stocks or mutual funds.

Rental Income—the net operating profit from any income producing property you own.

Other—any miscellaneous income not covered above.

FIXED EXPENSES

These payments must be made with regularity and, for the most part, will not fluctuate in the amount due.

Housing—rent or home mortgage payments.

Utilities—gas, water, electric, and telephone.

Loan payment—such as for an automobile, boat, etc.

Taxes—Federal and State Income Taxes—would be listed on your company withholding statement. If self-employed, check with your accountant.

Social Security Withholding —check with your employer or accountant for the exact figures.

Property Taxes —if you own a home, check your property tax bill.

22

FIXED EXPENSES (Continued)

Insurance—includes premiums for all insurance in force—life, disability, medical, auto, casualty.

Other—could include financial support to parents or children.

List any other obligation(s) not enumerated above.

VARIABLE EXPENSES

Payments are, to some degree, discretionary. You may elect to reduce, increase, or eliminate them as circumstances dictate.

Food—might be a good time to examine your eating habits.

Clothing—include dry cleaning, laundry and personal effects.

Travel—includes major trips such as to Hawaii or Europe as well as weekend excursions.

Recreation—entertainment, dining out, green fees (if you play golf), etc.

Household maintenance—includes the cost of cleaning service, pool service, gardener, window washing, etc.

Transportation—all costs related to motorized vehicles—cars, motorboats, motorbikes—includes gas, repairs, and license fees.

Education—cost of children's education or courses of study taken by you. Include tuition and cost of books.

Medical Expenses—all costs not covered by your medical or dental insurance policies.

Church and Charity—include cash contributions only.

Spending Money—pocket money, your weekly allowance.

Other—might also include such temporary expenses as a veterinarian's bill.

TOTAL THE FIXED AND VARIABLE EXPENSES, THEN SUBTRACT THIS TOTAL FROM YOUR TOTAL INCOME. HOPEFULLY, THERE IS A SURPLUS THAT CAN BE EARMARKED FOR THE ESTABLISHMENT OF A CASH RESERVE TO FUND A FUTURE PURCHASE (SUCH AS A CAR) OR INVESTMENTS.

In our sample on page 20, Charles and Barbara have a total income of $54,820. Their total (fixed and variable) expenses are $40,984. This leaves a surplus of $13,836 for the year to be invested, spent, or placed in savings.

THE BALANCE SHEET: AN X-RAY OF YOUR FINANCIAL CONDITION

A fundamental starting point in the financial planning process is the creation of a personal **Balance Sheet**. It measures your financial condition at a given point in time. In its simplest form, a balance sheet consists of:

A. ASSETS (WHAT YOU OWN)

B. LIABILITIES (WHAT YOU OWE)

C. NET WORTH—the difference between what you own and what you owe

REMEMBER: A − B = C

DISTINCTION BETWEEN AN INCOME STATEMENT AND
A BALANCE SHEET:

A BALANCE SHEET—PORTRAYS YOUR CURRENT FINANCIAL
CONDITION ON A GIVEN DATE SUCH AS
JANUARY 1, 19XX.

AN INCOME STATEMENT—PORTRAYS YOUR RECENT FINANCIAL
HISTORY. FOR EXAMPLE: FOR THE
PERIOD BEGINNING JANUARY 1, 19XX
AND ENDING DECEMBER 31, 19XX—A ONE
YEAR SPAN.

Before completing your Balance Sheet shown on the next page, study the sample Balance Sheet drawn up for Charles and Barbara Thomas on page 25 and carefully read the Balance Sheet instructions on pages 26 and 27.

THE BALANCE SHEET

BALANCE SHEET
(STATEMENT OF FINANCIAL CONDITION)
CURRENT DATE _____

ASSETS		**LIABILITIES**	
CURRENT ASSETS		**CURRENT LIABILITIES***	
Cash on hand	$_____	Unpaid Bills	_____
Checking Account	_____	Credit cards	_____
Savings Account	_____	Bank or Installment Loan	_____
Life Insurance Cash Values	_____	Residence Mortgage Loan	_____
Stocks/Bonds	_____	• Other	_____
Mutual Funds	_____	• Other	_____
• Other	_____	• Other	_____
• Other	_____		
Total	$_____	Total	$_____
REAL ESTATE/INVESTMENTS		**LONG TERM LIABILITIES**	
Residence	_____	Bank or Installment Loan	_____
Rental Income Property	_____	Residence Mortgage Loan	_____
Real Estate Limited		• Other	_____
Partnerships	_____	• Other	_____
• Other	_____	• Other	_____
• Other	_____	• Other	_____
Total	$_____		
		Total	$_____
PERSONAL ASSETS			
Automobiles	_____		
Furniture & Household			
Accessories	_____		
Jewelry, Collections, Etc.	_____		
• Other	_____		
• Other	_____		
Total	$_____	**TOTAL LIABILITIES (B)**	$_____
RETIREMENT FUNDS			
IRA	_____		
Company Salary Savings			
(401(k))	_____		
Vested Pension Benefits	_____		
Annuities	_____		
• Other	_____		
• Other	_____		
Total	$_____		
		NET WORTH (C)	$_____
TOTAL ASSETS (A)	$ _____		

*PAYMENT DUE WITHIN NEXT 12 MONTH PERIOD.

(Sample)
BALANCE SHEET
(STATEMENT OF FINANCIAL CONDITION)

Charles and Barbara Thomas
CURRENT DATE <u>March 31, 19XX</u>

ASSETS

CURRENT ASSETS

Cash on hand	$ 350
Checking Account	1,300
Savings Account	2,000
Life Insurance Cash Values	1,500
Stocks/Bonds	2,500
Mutual Funds	1,000
• Other (U.S. Savings Bond)	5,000
• Other (Cert. of Deposit)	10,000
Total	$ 23,650

REAL ESTATE/INVESTMENTS

Residence	225,000
Rental Income Property	—
Real Estate Limited Partnerships	—
• Other	
• Other	
Total	$ 225,000

PERSONAL ASSETS

Automobiles	7,500
Furniture & Household Accessories	12,000
Jewelry, Collections, Etc.	3,500
• Other (Motor Home)	8,700
• Other	
Total	$ 31,700

RETIREMENT FUNDS

IRA	7,200
Company Salary Savings (401(k))	9,000
Vested Pension Benefits	20,000
Annuities	—
• Other	
• Other	
Total	$ 36,200

TOTAL ASSETS (A) $ 316,550

LIABILITIES

CURRENT LIABILITIES*

Unpaid Bills	550
Credit cards	1,100
Bank or Installment Loan	900
Residence Mortgage Loan	3,600
• Other	
• Other	
• Other	
Total	$ 6,150

LONG TERM LIABILITIES

Bank or Installment Loan	5,600
Residence Mortgage Loan	49,000
• Other	
• Other	
• Other	
• Other	
Total	$ 54,600

TOTAL LIABILITIES (B) $ 60,750

NET WORTH (C) $ 255,800

*PAYMENT DUE WITHIN NEXT 12 MONTH PERIOD.

INSTRUCTIONS TO SAMPLE BALANCE SHEET

CURRENT ASSETS

Cash On Hand—include the cash in your wallet, cookie jar, and/or mattress.

Checking Account—could also be a money market account or money fund with check writing privileges. Use current balances.

Savings Account—use current balance.

Life Insurance Cash Values—to find the current guaranteed cash values of your insurance policy, turn to the table printed in the policy itself (term policies have no cash value). The figures in the table are for each $1,000 of the face amount of the policy for each year of the policy's age. You should call your insurance agent if you encounter any problems.

Stock/Bonds—check the value in a newspaper such as the Wall Street Journal. Call your broker if a stock or bond is not listed. Multiply the number of shares owned by the current price. Enter total.

Mutual Funds—follow the same procedure as for stocks and bonds. Use the net asset value (NAV) for the price per share.

U.S. Savings Bonds—use the face value of the bonds you own (assuming you will hold them until maturity).

Certificate of Deposit—list the value of the Certificate at maturity (unless you plan to withdraw the funds earlier).

REAL ESTATE/INVESTMENTS

Residence—with the aid of a realtor, obtain the sales price of comparable properties in your area. You may also arrange for a written appraisal (which will cost you money).

Use the same procedure for any other real property that you own.

For an interest in a limited partnership, use the amount of your original investment.

PERSONAL ASSETS

Automobile (or any other motorized vehicle)—obtain wholesale blue book value or compare your vehicle with others like it in the classified ads of your local newspaper.

Personal Property—includes home furnishings, clothing, etc. For such items, assume no greater value than what someone would pay you if you were to sell the items today. In the case of precious stones, silver, china or a coin collection, you may want to have such items appraised. If such items are covered under a homeowner's or renter's policy, your insurance agent may be able to help you in this regard.

SAMPLE BALANCE SHEET (Continued)

RETIREMENT FUNDS

IRA—List the current value of all previous investments that you have made.

Company Salary Savings Plan (or other various retirement programs)—list the value that you are currently entitled to (your vested benefits).

Annuities—you can call your insurance agent to determine the current value or refer to the table in the policy itself.

CURRENT LIABILITIES

Unpaid Bills—list bills you know have to be paid in the next few months—an insurance premium, property tax bill, plumbing bill, department store accounts, etc.

Credit Cards—list current balance due on all charge cards.

Bank or Installment Loan—balance due within the next 12 month period. Auto loan, furniture, etc.

Residence Mortgage Loan—total of mortgage payments due within the next 12 months.

Other—might include money you owe your parents, personal friend, or business associate.

LONG TERM LIABILITIES

List the balance for all loans due in excess of 12 months. This would include the balance on various bank or installment loans as well as the balance due on your home mortgage.

NET WORTH OF CHARLES AND BARBARA THOMAS

Total Assets (A)

This is the sum total of current assets ($23,650), fixed assets—real estate/investments plus personal assets—($225,000 + $31,700 = $256,700) and retirement funds ($36,200). $23,650 + $256,700 + $36,200 = $316,550.

Total Liabilities (B)

This is the sum total of current liabilities ($6,150) and long term liabilities ($54,600). $6,150 + $54,600 = $60,750.

(A) − (B) = NET WORTH (C) OR

$316,550 − $60,750 = $255,800.

BUDGETING

A **budget** is a worksheet that describes your lifestyle (or standard of living).

Your budget is to your financial fitness program what your diet is to your physical fitness program. The primary objective of a budget is to improve your situation in the future with a system of **disciplined** spending.

To understand where you now are financially, where you are going and how you are going to get there, complete the income and expense worksheets on the following pages.

REMEMBER
INCOME STATEMENT—A REPORT ON YOUR PAST
BALANCE SHEET — A PICTURE OF THE PRESENT
BUDGET — A PLAN FOR YOUR FUTURE

DEVELOPING A BUDGET

BUDGET: PART I
INCOME FORECASTING

For purposes of forecasting, figure all sources of your income on a monthly basis. Then, forecast your average monthly income over the next year by completing the worksheets shown on the next two pages.

Use the following guidelines in the completion of this income forecast:

1. Enter the monthly income for each of the various categories listed.

2. Enter the total for each month at the bottom of the page.

3. Enter the total in each income category for the year in Column ''A''.

4. Divide Column ''A'' by 12 and enter the average for each month in Column ''B''.

INSTRUCTIONS FOR INCOME FORECASTING SHEET

Income forecasting is the first step in the budgeting process. On this sheet, you are to list all sources of income and when you anticipate receiving such income.

Wages or Salary—If paid monthly, list the gross amount of income.

Bonuses or Commissions—if you know you will receive a bonus a certain time of the year, list the anticipated amount in the appropriate monthly column.

Interest and Dividends—record the amounts and months when such income is anticipated.

Rental Income—may vary from month to month.

Annuities, pensions, social security—are usually paid monthly.

Other—list any other income not previously mentioned.

Before entering your figures for the Budget Worksheets Part I found on pages 30-31, review carefully the completed forms for Charles and Barbara Thomas on pages 32 and 33.

BUDGET: PART I
INCOME FORECASTING
DATE _____

Source	Jan.	Feb.	Mar.	Apr.	May	June
Husband's wages or salary						
Wife's wages or salary						
Bonuses or commissions						
Interest Income						
Dividends						
Rental Income						
Annuities, pensions, Social Security						
Other						
TOTAL BY MONTH						

July	Aug.	Sept.	Oct.	Nov.	Dec.	Estimated 12-Month Total "A"	Monthly Average "B"

32

(Sample)
BUDGET: PART I
Charles and Barbara Thomas
INCOME FORECASTING

DATE <u>March 31, 19XX</u>

Source	Jan.	Feb.	Mar.	Apr.	May	June
Husband's wages or salary	3,000	3,000	3,000	3,000	3,000	3,000
Wife's wages or salary	1,500	1,500	1,500	1,500	1,500	1,500
Bonuses or commissions						
Interest Income	60	60	60	60	60	60
Dividends				50		
Rental Income						
Annuities, pensions, Social Security						
Other						
TOTAL BY MONTH	4,560	4,560	4,560	4,610	4, 560	4,560

July	Aug.	Sept.	Oct.	Nov.	Dec.	Estimated 12-Month Total "A"	Monthly Average "B"
3,000	3,000	3,000	3,000	3,000	3,000	36,000	3,000
1,500	1,500	1,500	1,500	1,500	1,500	18,000	1,500
60	60	60	60	60	60	720	60
			50			100	8
4,560	4,560	4,560	4,610	4,560	4,560	54,820	4,568

BUDGET: PART II
EXPENSE FORECASTING

If you wish to keep the same lifestyle as in previous months—at least in some categories—review your past expenditures (see your completed Income or Cash Flow Statement). You can then better estimate what amounts to enter in your Budget: Part II.

Use the following guidelines in the completion of this expense forecast:

1. For categories such as medical insurance premiums, write in the amount if you pay it, or write ''paid by employer'', if that is applicable. Similarly, for taxes, you may write ''withheld by employer''.

2. Enter monthly expenses for each of the categories listed.

3. Enter a total for each month at the bottom of the page.

4. Enter the total in each expense category for the year in Column A.

5. Divide Column A by 12 and enter the average for each month in Column B.

As earlier, it would be helpful to look at the completed worksheets for Charles and Barbara Thomas (pages 38 and 39) before beginning work on yours.

POINTS TO PONDER

Can the total monthly spending be accommodated by your average monthly income? If not, start making some priority decisions. Where can you make adjustments? What (variable) expenditures can be postponed or reduced? Remember, the budgeting process will require sacrifice and compromises. It is best to resolve any potential deficits before the money is actually spent.

INSTRUCTIONS TO SAMPLE EXPENSE FORECASTING

Housing—Rent/Mortgage Payments. Reflect any future increase or decrease due to a move, refinancing, etc.

Housing—Repairs/Improvements. You may wish to include a figure in Column A which will serve as a contingency fund or reserve.

Utilities—includes gas, electric, water, and telephone. Make seasonal adjustments for increased air conditioning or heating needs.

Food—also include household items such as paper towels, soap, pet food, etc.

Medical—Premiums. If coverage is provided by your employer, write ''Covered by Employer''.

Medical—Doctor, Dentist, Drugs, and Hospital. You may wish to put a total in Column A serving as a contingency or reserve fund. This would cover the deductible and co-insurance factor contained in your medical policy.

Clothing—If you are fairly consistent in the amount that you spend, fill in an average monthly figure. Otherwise, establish a reserve fund in Column A.

Transportation—You may wish to average the costs on a monthly basis. In the example on pages 38-39, we are showing quarterly insurance premium payments. Include monthly charges for gas, oil, and repairs. A review of previous records should give you a fairly accurate monthly figure.

Recreation/Entertainment—You will note the June figure (page 39) is substantially higher than the other months. This is in anticipation of a vacation in June.

Personal Improvement—List all magazine subscriptions, health club dues, tuition, etc.

Short Term Funding—If you are currently paying for major household items such as a refrigerator, list the monthly payments you are making.

Savings and Investment—In our example on pages 38-39, the Thomases are making an IRA contribution in April, and plan to invest $8,654 in the month of December. If you are on a systematic investment program, put in your monthly figure.

Spending Money—Record the amount of cash you carry and spend monthly.

Gifts—If a family wedding is anticipated or a special birthday celebration, estimate the costs of that specific occasion. Otherwise, a monthly average figure should be used.

Church and Charity—Indicate the frequency of contributions that are made. In the sample, the Thomases elect to make cash contributions twice a year, once in June and once in December.

Life Insurance—List all premium payments (monthly, quarterly, etc.).

Taxes—If Federal and State Income Taxes are withheld by your employer, write ''Withheld by Employer'' and record the total.

Miscellaneous—List any other anticipated expense not enumerated above.

BUDGET: PART II
EXPENSE FORECASTING
DATE _____

Expense Category	Explanation of Categories	Jan.	Feb.	Mar.
Housing	Rent, mortgage payments, insurance, and taxes			
	Repairs and improvements			
Utilities	Gas, electric, water, telephone			
Food				
Medical	Premiums			
	Doctor, dentist, drugs, and hospital			
Clothing				
Transportation (all motorized vehicles)	Purchase payments, insurance and license fees			
	Gas, oil, repairs, parking, tolls, and so on			
Recreation and entertainment	Dining out, movies, vacations, etc.			
Personal improvement	Magazines and newspapers			
	Books and tuition			
Short-term funding	Purchase of a major appliance			
Savings and investment	For long-term goals: IRAs, Annuities, Stocks, Bonds, Mutual Funds			
Spending money	Cash carried in wallet			
Gifts	Weddings, birthdays, etc.			
Church and charity				
Life insurance				
Taxes				
Miscellaneous	Legal services, debt repayments, union dues, etc.			
TOTAL				

Apr.	May	June	July	Aug.	Sept.	Oct.	Nov.	Dec.	Estimated 12 Month Total "A"	Monthly Average "B"

38

(Sample)
BUDGET: PART II
Charles and Barbara Thomas
EXPENSE FORECASTING

DATE March 31, 19XX

Expense Category	Explanation of Categories	Jan.	Feb.	Mar.
Housing	Rent, mortgage payments, insurance and taxes	579	579	579
	Repairs and improvements			
Utilities	Gas, electric, water, telephone	63	63	63
Food		433	433	433
Medical	Premiums			
	Doctor, dentist, drugs and hospital			
Clothing				
Transportation (all motorized vehicles)	Purchase payments, insurance and license fees			250
	Gas, oil, repairs, parking, tolls and so on	104	104	104
Recreation and entertainment	Dining out, movies, vacations, etc.	92	92	92
Personal improvement	Magazines and newspapers			
	Books and tuition			
Short-term funding	Purchase of a major appliance			
Savings and investment	For long-term goals: IRAs, Annuities, Stocks, Bonds, Mutual Funds			
Spending money	Cash carried in wallet	200	200	200
Gifts	Weddings, Birthdays, etc.			
Church and charity				
Life insurance		45	45	45
Taxes				
Miscellaneous	Legal services, debt repayments, union dues, etc.	500	500	500
TOTAL		2,016	2,016	2,266

* A contingency fund for the year.
** Total By Month—January-December = $51,220
 + Contingency funds (medical/clothing) + 3,600
  Estimated 12 Month Total "A" $54,820

Apr.	May	June	July	Aug.	Sept.	Oct.	Nov.	Dec.	Estimated 12 Month Total "A"	Monthly Average "B"
579	579	579	579	579	579	579	579	579	6,948	579
63	63	63	63	63	63	63	63	63	756	63
433	433	433	433	433	433	433	433	433	5,196	433
COVERED BY EMPLOYER										
									600*	50
									3,000*	250
		250			250			250	1,000	83
104	104	104	104	104	104	104	104	104	1,248	104
92	92	2,092	92	92	92	92	92	92	3,104	259
2,000								8,654	10,654	888
200	200	200	200	200	200	200	200	200	2,400	200
		400						400	800	67
45	45	45	45	45	45	45	45	45	540	45
WITHHELD BY EMPLOYER									12,574	1,048
500	500	500	500	500	500	500	500	500	6,000	500
4,016	2,016	4,666	2,016	2,016	2,266	2,016	2,016	11,320	54,820**	4,568

THE ROLE OF INSURANCE IN FINANCIAL PLANNING

The fundamental objective of insurance is to provide a means to offset the burden of financial loss. Think of insurance as an alternative method of dealing with risk. You are paying an insurance premium (small cost) to avoid paying the total cost for a catastrophic loss (such as your house burning down).

A sound insurance program should answer the "what if's" in your life. For example:

What if you were faced with a major medical expense? (health insurance)

What if you were unable to work for a long period of time due to a severe illness or accident? (disability insurance)

What if someone injured themselves on your property? (homeowner's insurance)

What if a fire destroyed many of your personal possessions? (homeowner's insurance)

What if you were involved in a severe automobile accident? (auto insurance)

What if you were to die tomorrow? (life insurance)

THE ROLE OF INSURANCE IN FINANCIAL PLANNING (continued)

Insurance affects everyone. Few people could own their own home, drive a car, attain adequate medical attention or provide financial security for their family without it. By providing the means to help people accomplish their goals without fear of catastrophic loss, insurance can improve the quality of life. It is, therefore, important to be aware of the major types of insurance coverage.

Life Insurance—provides a lump sum payment (or sometimes a series of payments) in the event of the death of the family breadwinner.

Disability Insurance—provides a monthly income benefit in the event the family breadwinner is disabled (unable to work) because of an accident or long term illness.

Medical (health) Insurance—provides for coverage in the event of hospitalization and medical expenses arising from injury or sickness.

Property, Casualty, and Liability Insurance—provides protection from the claims of others as well as the loss of personal property. Most typical policies are automobile and homeowners/renters. Each provides a variety of coverages.

Some insurance protection in each of the above areas is important. In some cases, an employer may provide group life, disability and/or health insurance. Typically, liability insurance such as automobile insurance, must be acquired on an individual basis.

Please take the time to complete the insurance checklist on page 42 and then review all of your various insurance policies (both personal and group—those provided by your employer). Then complete the worksheets on pages 52 thru 57. The intent is to make you aware of the types of insurance coverage you have in force. *Don't* spend time analyzing each policy, but *do* record the basic information on each.

Author's Note

When you meet with an insurance agent to review your insurance program, you should:

- ask about an umbrella policy—one which offers coverage after the limits of your automobile and/or homeowners/renters policies have been exhausted.

- discuss premium savings that would occur if you increased your deductibles.

- ask how to protect yourself from uninsured or underinsured motorists.

INSURANCE CHECK LIST

To help you focus on your insurance needs, complete the following check list.

Yes   No

☐   ☐   I am aware of and have considered the four basic forms of insurance protection:

- Life—   Protection against financial disruption in the event of my death, or that of my spouse.

- Disability—   Protection against the loss of my ability to produce income (economic death).

- Medical (health)—   Protection against prolonged illness or severe injury.

- Property, Casualty & Liability—   Protection against personal losses, lawsuits, property damage, and automobile accidents.

☐   ☐   I have given some thought to the four basic methods of managing risk.

- Avoidance of risk—   If I don't drive a car, I can't be the driver involved in a traffic accident.

- Reduction or prevention of risk—   If I remove combustible materials from my garage, I minimize the risk of fire.

- Assumption or retention of risk—   I assume greater risk by choosing a larger deductible for my insurance policy. (The trade off is a lower premium rate).

- Transfer of risk—   If I buy insurance, the insurance company would incur all losses once the deductible has been satisfied.

☐   ☐   I plan to evaluate annually:

- all of my insurance coverage to prevent gaps or duplication.

- to replace or update policies on the basis of cost and coverage.

A FLEXIBLE MONEY INSTRUMENT: LIFE INSURANCE

WHAT LIFE INSURANCE PROVIDES

Life insurance is the only instrument that can provide living benefits or become self-completing upon death. Life insurance is an important part of your total financial picture.

Life insurance provides a source of instant and tax-free liquidity (income). Such liquidity is very important in the early stages of family and economic development and can also help protect accumulated wealth in later years by providing an instant source of (tax-free) cash.

TWO BASIC KINDS OF LIFE INSURANCE

TERM—Provides protection only for a specified term or period of time. The policy pays off only in the event you die. It is the cheapest form of insurance protection in terms of initial premium payments, but not necessarily the most cost effective form of insurance in the long run.

PERMANENT—Protection is provided for the life-time of the insured. Other names for permanent insurance include: whole life, interest sensitive, or universal life insurance. Such policies have a cash value (savings) feature. The cash values accumulate on a tax deferred basis at a very competitive rate—currently 8-10%. The present-day policies are structured to allow the premiums to "vanish" in a relatively short period of time—7-10 years.

BENEFITS OF CASH VALUE ORIENTED LIFE INSURANCE

- Cash values accumulate tax free—usually at a very competitive interest rate.

- The owner may borrow funds from the policy on a tax free basis (given certain circumstances under current legislation).

- The death benefit is paid to the beneficiary free of income taxes.

- The death benefit avoids probate.

- Limited number of premium payments based upon age and the amount of insurance applied for.

LIFE INSURANCE—
EXAMPLE OF CASH ORIENTED INSURANCE

To demonstrate both the life and death benefits of the present-day insurance policies, consider the case of Jason White who is 40 years old. He has a wife and three young children.

Jason wants an insurance plan that will provide ample protection for his family and the opportunity for supplemental income beginning at age 55.

His cash flow will allow him to spend approximately $200 a month in premium which will provide the following policy:

END OF YEAR	AGE	ANNUAL OUTLAY	LOANS AND WITHDRAWALS*	NET DEATH BENEFIT	NET ACCUMULATED VALUE
1	40	$2,500	$ 0	$210,000	$ 2,188
2	41	2,500	0	210,000	4,561
3	42	2,500	0	210,000	7,138
4	43	2,500	0	210,000	9,936
5	44	2,500	0	210,000	13,008
6	45	2,500	0	210,000	16,382
7	46	2,500	0	210,000	20,093
8	47	0	0	210,000	21,419
9	48	0	0	210,000	22,872
10	49	0	0	210,000	24,470
11	50	0	0	210,000	26,228
12	51	0	0	210,000	28,163
13	52	0	0	210,000	30,294
14	53	0	0	210,000	32,647
15	54	0	0	210,000	35,178
16	55	0	3,350(L)	54,082	34,877
17	56	0	3,350(L)	53,767	34,539
18	57	0	3,350(L)	53,212	34,162
19	58	0	3,350(L)	52,397	33,743
20	59	0	3,350(L)	51,300	33,279
21	60	0	3,350(L)	50,047	32,880
22	61	0	3,350(L)	49,708	32,443
23	62	0	3,350(L)	49,210	31,966
24	63	0	3,350(L)	48,537	32,443
25	64	0	3,350(L)	47,674	30,871
26	65	0	3,350(L)	46,603	30,246
27	66	0	3,350(L)	46,179	29,560
28	67	0	3,350(L)	45,626	28,807
29	68	0	3,350(L)	44,931	27,982
30	69	0	3,350(L)	44,081	27,077

(L) = Tax-Free Loan   * = Withdrawals could continue PAST AGE 80.

To better assess your requirements, complete the life insurance needs analysis on page 48 and 49. But first, review the completed sample of the life insurance needs analysis on pages 52 through 54.

EXAMPLE OF CASH ORIENTED INSURANCE (Continued)

Summary of Benefits:

1. Jason will pay a total premium over a 7-year period of $17,500.00

2. The initial amount of insurance purchased was   210,000.00

3. Beginning at age 55 and for each of the next 20 years, he can withdraw $3,500.00 tax free for a total of   52,500.00

4. At age 70, the net death benefit would be   44,081.00

5. The net amount of cash remaining in the policy at age 70 would be   27,077.00

Author's Note:

To obtain a more complete and detailed insurance illustration, you should contact your insurance agent or financial advisor.

TAX FACT

As a result of the Technical and Miscellaneous Revenue Act of 1988 (TNRA 88), all Single Premium Whole Life Policies issued after June 20, 1988, will continue to receive tax deferred accumulations, a tax free death benefit, *but not* tax free policy loans. Any withdrawals will be treated as ordinary income. Furthermore, these distributions will be subject to a 10% penalty if taken prior to age 59½.

LIFE INSURANCE—
BUSINESS PLANNING APPLICATIONS

Pension and Profit Sharing Plans—Qualified Retirement Plans—are burdened with a crushing load of rules and regulations. The strict compliance rules and administrative costs associated with such plans can be avoided through the use of a Whole Life or Universal Life Insurance Policy.

Advantages of using life insurance:

1. Like funds in a retirement plan, the premiums paid to the insurance company build up tax free.

2. If an employee dies prior to retirement, the policy pays off as a nontaxable death benefit.

3. Payments to a retired employee by a qualified retirement plan are fully taxable, but withdrawals from a life insurance policy can be tax free by borrowing the accumulated cash values.

Application No. 1:   *Traditional split dollar insurance*

SITUATION

Alex is a Vice President for Vortex, a small paper company. He has expressed a desire to have more life insurance protection for his family.

SOLUTION:

Vortex can purchase a life insurance contract (with a vanishing premium) on Alex's life. Vortex pays the bulk of the premium (equal to the annual cash value build-up). Alex is the owner of the policy. Alex's beneficiaries would receive the policy's proceeds (less all premiums paid by the company) in the event of his death while still employed. Alex would pay a small cost for the insurance based upon either IRS set rates or the insurance company's standard term insurance rate.

BUSINESS PLANNING APPLICATIONS
(Continued)

Application No. 2:   *Reverse Split Dollar Situation*

SITUATION:

John works for a small manufacturing company that has a modest pension plan. The company would like to increase John's retirement benefits, but because of anti-discrimination laws, can't increase his benefits without raising the benefits of everyone on the payroll.

SOLUTION

The company agrees to pay the premiums for an insurance contract with John as the Insured and owner of the policy (including all of the accumulated cash values).

The company will be the beneficiary during John's working years. The policy can be structured so that by the time John retires, the premiums will have vanished. The beneficiary is then changed to John's designee. John would thus have accumulated cash values to supplement his retirement income.

Application No. 3:   *Deferred Compensation Situation*

SITUATION

Mark is a highly salaried Executive Vice President for a large publicly traded corporation. He does not need all of his annual income and would like to reduce his current income tax liability.

The company would like to reward Mark for his contributions to the company as a key employee. A supplemental executive retirement plan has been considered.

SOLUTION:

The company enters into a formal agreement with Mark to defer a portion of his annual income (say, $10,000). In conjunction with this agreement, a life insurance contract is purchased on the life of Mark by the company. If Mark dies while employed, his beneficiaries receive the death benefit, tax free. When Mark retires, he receives the cash values from the insurance contract to supplement other retirement income. Effectively, the amount of retirement income paid out is equal to the amount of money deferred.

LIFE INSURANCE NEEDS

DATE _____

CAPITAL NEEDS

Funeral expenses $_____
Final expenses (current bills)   _____
Medical expenses not covered
  by insurance   _____
Estate taxes   _____
Attorney and court fees   _____
Emergency fund   _____
Pay-off mortgage balance   _____
Education fund   _____
Other   _____

TOTAL CAPITAL NEEDS $_____ (A)

CAPITAL AVAILABLE

Liquid assets $_____
  (checking and savings)
Existing insurance proceeds*
  (company insurance and
  personal policies if paid
  in lump-sum)   _____
Death benefits of retirement
  programs (if paid in
  lump-sum)   _____
Other   _____

TOTAL CAPITAL AVAILABLE $_____ (B)

ANNUAL INCOME NEEDS OF SURVIVORS

Spouse, children $_____
Other (parents)   _____

TOTAL ANNUAL INCOME NEEDS $_____ (C)

*Proceeds can be taken in a lump sum or in installment payments.

LIFE INSURANCE NEEDS (Continued)

ANNUAL INCOME AVAILABLE TO SURVIVORS

Social Security survivors' benefits $_____

Survivors' benefit from retirement
   programs (if paid in installments)   _____

Spouse's wage   _____

Income from investments   _____

Other (teenage children, veterans)   _____

TOTAL ANNUAL INCOME AVAILABLE $_____ (D)

CALCULATIONS TO DETERMINE TOTAL AMOUNT OF LIFE INSURANCE NEEDED

1. Total Capital Needs $_____ (A)
    Less Total Capital Available   −_____ (B)

    = Net Capital Needs-------------------- $_____ (E)

2. Total Annual Income Needs $_____ (C)
    Less Total Annual Income Available   −_____ (D)

    = Net Annual Income Needs -------- $_____ (F)

3. Additional Capital Needed $_____ (G)
    Divide (F) by the return assumed
    on the invested capital*

4. Total Additional Life Insurance
    Needed (Add (E) and (G)) $_____

*For example, at an annual return of 10%, you would need $90,000 to generate an annual income of $9,000. At an 8% annual return, you would need $112,500 to generate the same annual income of $9,000. ($9,000 ÷ .08 = $112,500).

INSTRUCTIONS TO LIFE INSURANCE NEEDS

CAPITAL NEEDS

Funeral Expenses—You will need to estimate. A reasonable figure might be $5,000.

Final Expenses—Current bills that must be paid—charge accounts, etc.

Medical Expenses—Those not ordinarily covered by insurance.

Estate Taxes—Costs will vary from state to state. It's best to consult with an estate planning attorney or financial planner for assistance.

Attorney & Court Fees—Seek assistance as noted above.

Emergency Fund—Estimate a minimum of three months fixed living expenses.

Pay-Off Mortgage Balance—If this is desirable, list current balance.

Education Fund—Estimate the amount necessary to complete four years of college for each child.

Other—Would include a major expense or debt not mentioned above (i.e., pay-off auto loan).

CAPITAL AVAILABLE

Liquid Assets—Total of funds in savings and checking accounts.

Existing Insurance Proceeds—List total of all insurance proceeds from either group (employer paid plans) or individual policies.

Death Benefits—Includes IRAs and company retirement plans that make a lump sum distribution in the event of death.

Other—Would include help from relatives or investments that could be liquidated such as stocks and bonds.

ANNUAL INCOME NEEDS

Spouse, Children—Estimate the amount necessary to maintain a comfortable standard of living.

Other—Estimate amount needed to support a parent or relative.

ANNUAL INCOME AVAILABLE

Social Security Survivors' Benefits—Your local social security office can provide you with this information.

Survivors' Benefit from Retirement Programs—if benefits are paid in installments rather than a lump sum, list the annual amount.

Spouse's Wage—If surviving spouse is employed, list annual income.

Income from Investments—Interest, dividends, etc.

Other—Any other source of income such as veteran's benefits or money earned by teenage children.

CALCULATIONS

1. Total Capital Needs—Take the Total Capital Needs (A) and subtract the Total Capital Available (B) which will equal Net Capital Needs (E).

2. Total Annual Income Needs—Take Total Annual Income Needs (C) and subtract Annual Income Available (D) which will equal Annual Income Needs (F).

3. Additional Capital Needed—Divide the Net Annual Income Needs (F) by the interest rate you assume you could receive on your investments. The lower the assumed interest rate, the greater amount of investment funds needed.

4. Total Additional Life Insurance Needed—By adding Net Capital Needs (E) and Additional Capital Needed (G) you will arrive at a figure representing the amount of insurance (if any) needed to make-up the shortage or deficiency in capital to maintain an adequate standard of living and provide for those things requiring a significant cash outlay.

Author's Note:

The type of insurance which you should purchase (either term or permanent)—is up to you—but you should have a clear understanding of the cost versus benefit of the insurance plan you select.

(SAMPLE)
CHARLES & BARBARA THOMAS
(ASSUME CHARLES DIES FIRST)
LIFE INSURANCE NEEDS

DATE ___3/31/XX___

CAPITAL NEEDS

Funeral expenses	$ 5,000
Final expenses (current bills)	6,150
Medical expenses not covered by insurance	1,500
Estate taxes	10,000
Attorney and court fees	2,500
Emergency fund	7,395
Pay off mortgage balance	49,000
Education fund	80,000
Other	5,600

TOTAL CAPITAL NEEDS $ 167,145 (A)

CAPITAL AVAILABLE

Liquid assets (checking and savings)	$ 3,300
Existing insurance proceeds* (company insurance and personal policies if paid in lump-sum)	150,000
Death benefits of retirement programs (if paid in lump-sum)	36,200
Other	—

TOTAL CAPITAL AVAILABLE $ 189,500 (B)

ANNUAL INCOME NEEDS OF SURVIVORS

Spouse, children	$ 25,000
Other (parents)	—

TOTAL ANNUAL INCOME NEEDS $ 25,000 (C)

ANNUAL INCOME AVAILABLE TO SURVIVORS

Social Security survivors' benefits	$ 5,000
Survivors' benefit from retirement programs (if paid in installments)	—
Spouse's wage	18,000
Income from investments	820
Other (teenage children, veterans)	—

TOTAL ANNUAL INCOME AVAILABLE $ 23,820 (D)

*Proceeds can be taken in a lump sum or in installment payments.

CALCULATIONS TO DETERMINE TOTAL AMOUNT OF LIFE INSURANCE NEEDED

1. Total Capital Needs $ ___167,145___ (A)
 Less Total Capital Available – ___189,500___ (B)
 = Net Capital Needs-------------------- $ ___-0-___ (E) Surplus of $22,355

2. Total Annual Income Needs $ ___25,000___ (C)
 Less Total Annual Income Available – ___23,820___ (D)
 = Net Annual Income Needs -------- $ ___1,180___ (F)

3. Additional Capital Needed $ ___14,750___ (G)
 Divide (F) by the return assumed
 on the invested capital

4. Total Additional Life Insurance
 Needed (Add (E) and (G)) $ ___-0-___

CALCULATIONS TO DETERMINE TOTAL AMOUNT OF LIFE INSURANCE NEEDED

1. Total Capital Needs

   In the preceding illustration, the Total Capital Available is greater than the Total Capital Needs. Under Net Capital Needs, there is actually a surplus of $22,355.

2. Total Annual Income Needs

   The Net Annual Income Needs is very small: $1,180.

3. Additional Capital Needed

   $1,180 (F) divided by an assumed rate of return of 8% would equal Additional Capital Needed of $14,750.

4. Additional Life Insurance Needed

   In this case, no additional insurance is needed. Why? Because (E) $22,355 represents a surplus and (G) $14,750 is less than the surplus figure.

Factors which could have changed the situation would include a larger mortgage, Barbara not remaining gainfully employed, or less insurance in force at Charles' death. In otherwords, each individual situation is unique and must be carefully evaluated.

INSTRUCTIONS TO SAMPLE LIFE INSURANCE NEEDS

CAPITAL NEEDS

Funeral expenses—estimated at $5,000.

Final expenses—include credit card balances and outstanding loans due in the next 12 months.

Medical (health) expenses—allowances made for the fact that the existing insurance will not pick up 100% of all medical bills.

Estate taxes—estimated at $10,000.*

Attorney & court fees—estimated at $2,500.*

Emergency fund—provision is made for 3 months fixed living expenses ($29,584 ÷ 12 = $2,465/mo. × 3 mos. = $7,395).

Pay-off mortgage balance—in this case, it has been decided that the existing mortgage balance of $49,000 would be paid in the event of Charles' death.

Education fund—it has been assumed that both children would graduate from college and the cost would be $40,000 for each child.

Other—here you would make allowances for any other capital expenditures that would be needed, such as bank or installment loans or paying off a loan made by a friend or relative.

CAPITAL AVAILABLE

Liquid assets—the total amount currently in all checking and savings accounts.

Existing insurance proceeds—in this case, Charles has a $100,000 group insurance policy paid for by his employer and a $50,000 whole life policy on which he pays the premiums.

Death benefits—represents the sum total of Charles' five IRA accounts and the vested portion of his company retirement funds.

Other—would include help from relatives, investments that could be readily liquidated, etc.

ANNUAL INCOME NEEDS OF SURVIVORS

Spouse, children—it has been estimated that Barbara will need an annual income of $25,000 to maintain a comfortable standard of living for her and the two children.

ANNUAL INCOME AVAILABLE TO SURVIVORS

Social Security Survivors' Benefits**—annual benefits have been estimated at $5,000 for the two minor children till age 18. Barbara does not qualify because her earned income exceeds $6,000 per year.

Survivors' benefit from retirement programs—all survivor benefits, in this case, are paid in lump sum.

Spouse's wage—Barbara has decided that she would continue to work in the event of Charles' death.

Income from investments—is a combination of interest and dividends on the current investments of the Thomas family.

Other—might include veteran's benefits, income generated by teenage children, help from relatives, etc.

---

*These figures can be obtained by consulting with an estate planning attorney or financial planner.

**These figures may be obtained by calling your local social security office.

INSURANCE COVERAGE SUMMARY

List the amount of insurance protection provided by each policy.

LIFE INSURANCE COVERAGE	(self)	(spouse)	Annual cost
Company Group Life Insurance	$_____	$_____	$_____
Travel Accident Insurance	_____	_____	_____
Accidental Death & Dismemberment Insurance (AD&D)	_____	_____	_____
Personal Life Insurance	_____	_____	_____
Policy # _____	_____	_____	_____
Policy # _____	_____	_____	_____
Policy # _____	_____	_____	_____
TOTAL	_____	_____	_____

DISABILITY COVERAGE			
Group Long Term Disability	_____	_____	_____
Individual Disability Programs	_____	_____	_____
Policy # _____	_____	_____	_____
Policy # _____	_____	_____	_____

MEDICAL (HEALTH) COVERAGE			
Company Medical Plan—Self	_____	_____	_____
Company Medical Plan—Spouse	_____	_____	_____
Individual Medical Coverage	_____	_____	_____
Policy # _____	_____	_____	_____
Policy # _____	_____	_____	_____

HOMEOWNERS/RENTERS COVERAGE			
Personal Property	_____	_____	_____
Fire	_____	_____	_____
Liability	_____	_____	_____
Policy # _____	_____	_____	_____

AUTO COVERAGE			
Liability	_____	_____	_____
Collision	_____	_____	_____
Comprehensive	_____	_____	_____
Other	_____	_____	_____
Policy # _____	_____	_____	_____

SECTION III

AN Rx FOR INVESTMENT AND TAX PLANNING

Making Your Money Work For You

MAKING YOUR MONEY WORK FOR YOU

You have just completed Step 1 (Examine) and Step 2 (Diagnose) in the financial planning process. You are now ready for Step 3 (Prescribe). The concepts and principles of investing discussed in this section may be considered a prescription to aid in the improvement of your financial health.

No one financial prescription is right for everyone, just as no single medical prescription can be applied with equal results. Once a recommended action is taken, it is important to monitor the results (Step 4) and make any adjustments that may be necessary on a regular basis.

An I.D.E.A.L. investment portfolio would contain the following prescribed ingredients:

a) Income (bank account interest; stock dividends; municipal bond interest)

b) Deductions (an IRA; your home mortgage interest payment)

c) Equity buildup—(mortgage reduction on your home or income producing property)

d) Appreciation (increase in stock prices)

e) Liquidity (easily convertible to cash in an emergency—money market funds, savings accounts, stocks)

Everyone would like a good return on their investments. What constitutes a good return depends on several things: your personal circumstances, your tolerance for risk, and the characteristics of a given investment (such as liquidity, capital appreciation or tax deferral).

There is no single best or perfect investment. Each has strengths and weaknesses that must be considered in light of your particular needs. For example, you must consider whether you are willing to risk a loss of principal for the possibility of a higher gain.

The two basic categories of investments are growth and income. Generally there is more risk associated with growth oriented investments (i.e., a share of stock) than with income oriented investments (i.e., savings account).

Income oriented prescriptions (i.e., R_{xs}) would include U.S. government securities, annuities, municipal bonds, cash value life insurance policies, money market funds, savings accounts, and/or certificates of deposit.

Growth oriented R_{xs} would include: stocks, corporate bonds, mutual funds, and/or real estate.

Speculative investments (which offer growth opportunities but also substantial risk) include: commodity trading (precious metals, pork bellies, etc.), equipment leasing, research & development programs, raw land, oil and gas exploration and some types of limited partnerships.

Note: For an overview, see the Investment Chart and the accompanying glossary beginning on page 73.

Remember: Normally the greater the potential reward (gain), the greater the risk.

Caveat: Always obtain and read the prospectus (disclosure of investment information) before making your final decision on any investment.

The basic objective of investing is to earn the maximum possible rate of return on the funds you have to invest, that are consistent with your goals, objectives, and tolerance for risk. The following pages contain information about factors that will influence your investment decisions.

EIGHT FACTORS INFLUENCING YOUR INVESTMENT DECISIONS

A doctor, when diagnosing an ailment, must look at all the symptoms before prescribing the right medication. Conversely, before a specific investment can be selected (prescribed), you must consider its primary objective—income or growth—in light of your specific goals and your tolerance for risk.

Following are eight factors to consider before making an investment decision. After you have finished reading them, rate the factors in order of their importance to you with 1 being "Most Important" and 8 being "Least Important". Place a number in the box provided.

1. **SAFETY OF PRINCIPAL (ORIGINAL INVESTMENT CAPITAL) AND INCOME**

To determine the relative safety of any investment, you must first analyze four types of risk:

Financial Risk— Unfavorable business conditions may reduce or eliminate an expected return (i.e., a company goes bankrupt in which you owned a number of shares).

Market Risk— Price fluctuations due to changes in investor attitudes (i.e., your utility stock goes down because of the Three Mile Island scare).

Interest Rate Risk— Market prices for your bonds (fixed income securities) tend to move inversely with changes in the general level of interest rates—as interest rates rise, bond prices fall.

Purchase Power Risk— The negative effect of inflation on the future purchasing power of your investments (i.e., the earnings of your savings account are not an adequate hedge against inflation).

Are you willing to take greater risks for the possibility of a greater reward? It's important to understand (when making investment decisions) your tolerance for risk taking. How much investment risk are you willing to take?

Low _____ Moderate _____ High _____

Is the risk you are willing to take in keeping with your objectives?

☐ 2. **RATE OF RETURN—THE YIELD OR AMOUNT YOU EARN ON YOUR INVESTMENT**

- Your yield can come from a variety of investment returns, such as interest, dividends, rental income, or capital appreciation.

- Normally, the greater your yield, the greater your risk.

☐ 3. **TAXATION OF INCOME—YOUR YIELD AFTER TAXES**

Taxes and investments are inter-related. Just as you control your weight to maintain good health you can control to a large degree the amount of taxes that you pay with your investment strategies. Your investment choices will ultimately determine the taxes you pay or don't pay. It is the marginal tax rate (i.e., an individual's tax bracket) that often influences an investment decision.

For example, current yield (8%) multiplied by 100% minus your highest income tax bracket (30%) equals after—tax yield.

OR:

$0.08 \times (1.00 - .30)$
$= 0.08 \times (.70)$
$= .056$ or 5.6% return on your 8% current yield

IT'S WHAT YOU GET TO KEEP THAT COUNTS.

☐ 4. **MARKETABILITY—THE ABILITY TO FIND A READY MARKET IN WHICH YOU CAN SELL YOUR INVESTMENT**

For example, common stocks are easily sold; selling real estate is often slower and more difficult as is the sale of a business.

☐ 5. | **LIQUIDITY—THE ABILITY TO FIND A READY MARKET FOR YOUR INVESTMENT AND STABILITY OF THE PRICE YOU WILL RECEIVE**

The key is to get your money back, quickly and easily, without incurring a loss. You would expect to receive all of your original investment from a savings account, but probably less if you sold a volatile stock in a declining market.

☐ 6. | **DIVERSIFICATION—A DEFENSIVE OR CONSERVATIVE INVESTMENT POLICY DESIGNED TO REDUCE YOUR RISK OF LOSS**

For example, you can:

— diversify among several types of investments—real estate, common stocks and certificates of deposit.

— diversify within a particular type of investment—buy several different common stock issues.

— diversify according to maturity—buy bonds and certificates of deposit that have different maturity dates.

— diversify the timing of investments—rather than investing a lump sum, invest a small amount every month (systematic investing).

☐ 7. | **SIZE OF YOUR INVESTMENT**

Some investments require a minimum amount to be invested:

Savings Bank	Normally no minimum
Mutual funds	Normally $300 up
Real estate limited partnerships	Normally $2,500 up
Municipal Bond Funds	Normally $300 up

8. **EASE OF MANAGEMENT—THE AVOIDANCE OF WORRY OVER FLUCTUATIONS IN YOUR INVESTMENT RESULTS**

You may want to eliminate time and work involved in managing your investment. For example, a mutual fund offers professional management and diversification. This is not true if you own your own apartment complex which you personally manage.

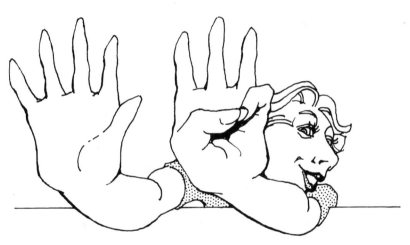

EIGHT INVESTMENT DECISION FACTORS

QUALIFIED RETIREMENT PLANS

One of the principal sources of retirement income, aside from social security, is from the retirement plans adopted by either a large corporation or small business owner.

Qualified plans by definition offer the following advantages:

1. Plan deposits (contributions) are deductible as a business expense. This is a strong motivation to establish a retirement plan.

2. Plan contributions are not currently taxable to employees, including owners/employers.

3. All funds, both contributions and earnings, accumulate tax free.

4. The income is taxed only as it is received (hopefully, when the employee is in a lower tax bracket).

If you are an employee of a corporation:

	YES	NO
1. Does your company offer any of the qualified plans listed on pages 65 or 66?	☐	☐
2. If so, are you an active participant (either making voluntary contributions or having them made for you by the company) of the plan?	☐	☐
3. Do you receive an annual valuation of your account balance in writing?	☐	☐
4. Do you know the projected value (in monthly income) at the time of your retirement?	☐	☐
5. If you are near retirement, do you understand the alternative ways of receiving your funds and the resultant tax consequences?	☐	☐

AUTHOR'S NOTE

Consult your employer regarding specific plan information. Most large corporations have an Employee Benefits section which handles the administration of all company retirement plans.

You may wish to consult your tax advisor or financial planner to determine the tax consequences of the various options available to you.

QUALIFIED PLANS

PLAN	DESCRIPTION	MAXIMUM ANNUAL CONTRIBUTIONS
IRA	Individual Retirement Account*	$2,000 or 100% of compensation whichever is less ($2,250 for a spousal IRA)
SEP	Simplified Employee Pension Consists of IRA's established by the employer for the employees Employer contributions are discretionary; same percentages must be allocated to each participant	15% of compensation or $30,000, whichever is less (Deductible employee contribution may not exceed $2,000)
TSA	Tax Shelter Annuity A retirement plan for employees of public school systems or non-profit organizations Funds are invested in life company annuity contracts	$9,500 or 20% of compensation, whichever is less Additional contributions allowable based upon length of employment and special catch-up provisions
401(k)	Employee sponsored savings plan Both employer and employee contributions are allowable Employer may match a certain portion of employee contributions. Percentage must be the same for all participants	Employee contribution is lesser of 25% of compensation or $7,313 Maximum allocation (which includes any employer contributions) to any participant is the lesser of $30,000 or 25% of the participant's compensation
Defined Contribution	A profit-sharing plan Annual employer contributions can vary—0 to 15% Percentage contributed by the employer must be the same for each employee	15% of compensation or $30,000, whichever is less

QUALIFIED PLANS (Continued)

PLAN	DESCRIPTION	MAXIMUM ANNUAL CONTRIBUTIONS
Defined Benefit	A pension plan The amount of income received at retirement is guaranteed by the plan An actuary is required to determine the actual contribution needed each year	$94,000 or 100% of compensation, whichever is less
Money Purchase Pension Plan	Allows for a higher percentage of contribution than the profit-sharing plan Once the contribution percent is selected, the employer must contribute the same percentage each year, regardless of company profits	25% of compensation or $30,000, whichever is less
Combined Profit Sharing and Money Purchase Plan	The employer can either contribute the full combined percentage of 25% or opt only for the required 10% of the Money Purchase Plan The profit-sharing contribution remains discretionary each year with a maximum of 15% of compensation	25% of compensation or $30,000, whichever is less

*See Appendix D on Page 122 to determine whether or not your contribution is tax deductible.

TAX FACTS

Contributions to a qualified plan (with the possible exception of the IRA under certain circumstances) are tax deductible.

Accumulations enjoy the advantage of compounding tax free.

Distributions are subject to ordinary income taxation. For information on the tax consequences of lump sum distributions, turn to Page 68.

IRA ROLLOVER A FLEXIBLE RETIREMENT PLANNING TOOL

WHAT IS IT?

A rollover is simply a transfer of money from one place to another. The IRA rollover account is also known as a Self-Directed Trust. Such an account or trust is established by you in your name. You may place into this account prior and/or future IRA contributions and your vested company retirement funds from such programs as the 401(k), ESOP, PAYSOP, profit sharing plan, and pension plan.

As long as you rollover your funds into the Self-Directed Trust within sixty (60) days of the date of distribution from the previous plan(s), you avoid paying taxes on the funds. All earnings on the funds in the Self-Directed Trust accumulate and compound tax free. No taxes are paid until money is withdrawn from the account. Withdrawals are subject to ordinary income taxation.

You control the account. You make all investment and withdrawal decisions. Funds withdrawn prior to age 59½ are subject to a 10% penalty (except in the event of disability). Systematic withdrawals must be made by age 70½ or be subject to a 50% tax. The minimum amount that must be withdrawn is determined each year based on your life expectancy and the life expectancy of your designated beneficiary, if applicable.

The administrator of the account can be a bank, stock brokerage firm, or an independent trust company. There is normally a small establishment fee and an annual administrative fee based upon the total value of the account. Usually, a quarterly report is provided showing the amount earned on each investment and the total value of the account.

HOW IT WORKS

Factual Situation

Sidney Gibson will retire in one year at age 65. He has IRA contributions which are in four different bank accounts. At retirement, Sidney will receive $50,000.00 in cash from his company's profit-sharing plan. He would like to have the IRA's and the company funds accumulate income until the maximum age of withdrawal (70½).

Steps to Take

1. Sidney should open a Self-Directed Trust account with the existing IRA's. The cash may then be invested in a variety of investment programs.

2. At retirement, he should roll over the company's funds ($50,000.00) into the Self-Directed Trust and invest the proceeds into investments best suited to his specific needs. All income generated by the investments in Sidney's account will accumulate and compound tax free.

TAXABILITY OF RETIREMENT DISTRIBUTIONS

There are three possible tax consequences regarding any planned distribution that you may receive:

1. Ordinary income taxation

   The taxable portion of the distribution* is added to ordinary income and is subject to federal and state income taxes.

2. Special 5- and 10-year averaging

   This tax is based on 5 or 10 times the amount that a single individual would pay on taxable income equal to 1/5 or 1/10 of the taxable lump sum. The 1986 Tax Tables are used. The lump sum is subject to both federal and state taxation.

   The 10-year method of averaging is available only to those who were age 50 or older as of January 1, 1986.

3. Rollover to an IRA

   The taxable portion may be rolled over to the IRA and thereby avoid the payment of any taxes until funds are withdrawn. Cash or stocks may be rolled over to this account.

   Any part not rolled over is taxed as ordinary income. The rollover must occur within 60 days of the date of distribution.

   Any withdrawals made prior to age 59½ are subject to a 10% penalty. Distributions must start by age 70½. All withdrawals are subject to ordinary income taxation.

AUTHOR'S NOTE

Employer sponsored programs are an integral and important part of an individual's finances. For an excellent supplement to the areas pertaining to employee benefits, send for *Financial Planning With Employee Benefits* by using the special order form on page 126 of this book.

After tax contributions are not subject to taxation.

TAXABILITY OF RETIREMENT DISTRIBUTIONS (Continued)

EXAMPLE OF A $100,000 TAXABLE DISTRIBUTION

	Ordinary Income*	5 Yr. Forward Average*	10 Yr. Forward Average*	IRA Rollover
Federal Income Taxes	$28,000	$16,400	$14,500	-0-
Remaining Balance	72,000	83,600	85,500	$100,000
8% Interest on Balance	5,760	6,688	6,840	8,000
Federal Taxes on Interest Income	1,613	1,873	1,915	-0-
Net Balance after Taxation	4,147	4,815	4,925	8,000

*A 28% federal tax rate has been assumed; state taxes are not included.

AUTHOR'S NOTE

Your taxable distributions are subject to federal and state income taxes. Taxes may be deferred by rolling over the distribution to an IRA. As an alternative, you may elect to pay the taxes at the time of distribution to take advantage of the special averaging rules. Consult your tax advisor or financial advisor to determine the most advantageous way to take your retirement plan distributions.

ANNUITIES

WHAT IS AN ANNUITY?

It is a contract issued by an insurance company. This contract can be purchased with a lump sum payment or a series of periodic payments. In return, the insurance company guarantees the purchaser of the contract (called the annuitant) periodic payments of principal and interest for either the annuitant's lifetime or for a specified period of time. The withdrawal of interest only is also an option.

WHAT ARE THE BENEFITS?

* *Safety.* Your principal and interest are guaranteed by a legal reserves insurance company. These types of insurance companies are required by law to establish reserves assuring the policyholder that the insurance company will have the assets which at least equal the future benefits provided by the policies.

* *Flexibility.* The annuitant decides when to take the income and therefore when to pay the taxes.

* *Interest accumulates on a tax deferred basis.* No taxes are paid until funds are received. Interest rates are very competitive and are usually guaranteed for a specific period of time.

* *The contract is free from probate.*

TYPES OF ANNUITY CONTRACTS

* *Single Premium Deferred Annuity*—requires a single premium payment. Interest accumulates and compounds on a tax deferred basis.

* *Flexible Premium Annuity*—after the initial premium payment, future payments—at some minimum amount—may be added to the contract.

* *Single Premium Immediate Annuity*—An annuity contract purchased with a lump sum. The annuitant immediately begins to receive income—usually monthly—for a specified period of time or for life. A portion of the payment is considered a return of principal and therefore is not subject to taxation.

ANNUITIES (Continued)

- *Variable Annuity*—May be purchased with a lump sum payment or a series of periodic payments. This type of annuity differs from the annuities enumerated above in only one aspect: Rather than receiving a guaranteed rate of return on your investment, your funds may be invested in a variety of investment vehicles such as Money Market Funds, stock or bond mutual funds, or U.S. Government Securities. At any given time, the total value of your annuity could be more or less than your original contribution, depending upon current market conditions. In the event of death, however, the beneficiary receives the original amount invested or the current value of the contract, whichever is greater. Therefore, the death benefit can never be less than the original amount invested.

POSSIBLE USES FOR THE ANNUITY CONTRACT

1. Building a supplemental retirement plan

2. Removing income from current taxation

3. Maximizing those situations calling for the safest way to accumulate the most money with government approved tax advantages

---

TAX FACT

Withdrawals from a deferred annuity contract are subject to ordinary income taxation. Withdrawals prior to age 59½ are subject to an additional 10% penalty.

INCOME ENHANCEMENT PROGRAM

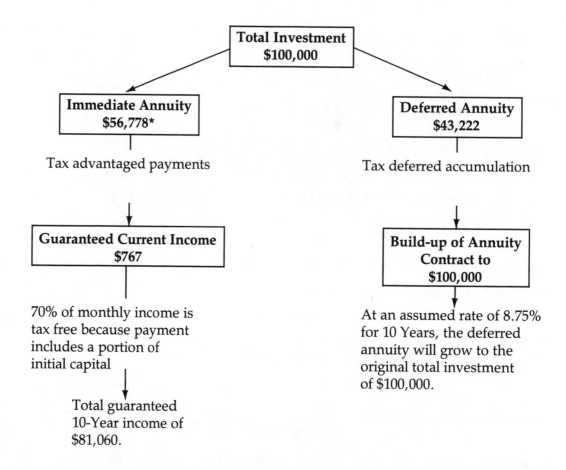

Total Investment
$100,000

Immediate Annuity
$56,778*

Deferred Annuity
$43,222

Tax advantaged payments

Tax deferred accumulation

Guaranteed Current Income
$767

Build-up of Annuity Contract to $100,000

70% of monthly income is tax free because payment includes a portion of initial capital

At an assumed rate of 8.75% for 10 Years, the deferred annuity will grow to the original total investment of $100,000.

Total guaranteed 10-Year income of $81,060.

POINT TO PONDER

Had the original $100,000 been placed in a 10-year, 8% Certificate of Deposit, the entire $80,000 of interest would have been taxed. However, only $24,300 is subject to taxation under the Income Enhancement Program. Assuming a 28% federal tax bracket, the tax savings would be $15,800 over the 10-year period. Less money to the government, more money to you!

---

*Based upon a male age 55: A 10-year annuity contract is purchased.—$100,000 was used for illustration purposes. A lesser amount may of course be used.

INVESTMENT CHART

A **SAVINGS** (CASH/LIQUIDITY)	B **INCOME** (CURRENT OR DEFERRED)	C **CAPITAL APPRECIATION** (LONG TERM GROWTH)	D **PRECIOUS METALS** (INFLATION HEDGES)

• **Life Insurance
  Cash Values**
 	
• **Savings Accounts**
 	
• **Money Market
  Accounts**
  Taxable
  Tax Exempt
 	
• **Certificates of
  Deposit**
	• **U.S. Savings Bonds**
	  Series EE or HH
	
	• **Annuities**
	
	• **Preferred Stocks**
	
	• **U.S. Government
	  Securities Funds**
	
	• **REITs**
	
	• **Income Funds**
	
	• **Bonds (Individual
	  or Mutual Funds)**
	  Municipal
	  Corporate
	  International
	
	• **All Cash Limited
	  Partnerships**
	  Oil/Gas
	  Real Estate
	  Equipment Leasing
	
	• **Utility Stocks**
		• **Individual Stocks**
		
		• **Growth Funds**
		
		• **Real Estate**
		  Individually
		  Owned
		  Limited Partnerships
		
		• **Raw Land**
			• **Gold**
			  Bullion Bars
			  Coins
			  Mutual Funds
			
			• **Silver**
			
			• **Platinum**

Risk/Reward Scale: Lower --- Higher

It is important to match as closely as possible the right investment with your investment objective.

Example:
John Larson, who is retired, wishes to generate additional, spendable income—with a minimum of risk—with the $10,000 that was part of a recent inheritance.

Wrong Type of Investment:
An aggressive growth fund—has long-term growth potential, but virtually no income.

Right Type of Investment:
Insured Money Market Fund—will provide income, safety, and liquidity.

INVESTMENT GLOSSARY

Annuity—A contract purchased from an insurance company. Interest is paid on the principal amount and accumulates tax free. Withdrawals are subject to taxation. Annuities are often used for retirement planning.

Appreciation—Increase in the dollar value of an asset (such as a share of stock) over time.

Bond—A debt instrument (liability) with a specified interest rate and maturity date. Issued by the government (federal, state, local) and agencies of the federal government and/or corporations.

Certificate of Deposit (C.D.)—A time deposit with a specified maturity date.

Common Stock—A security representing ownership in a corporation.

Inflation—The loss of purchasing power due to a general rise in prices (goods and services).

Investment Capital—Original amount invested.

Leverage—A magnification of the potential return (appreciation) on an investment. Often accomplished by controlling an asset with a relatively small amount of invested capital.

Limited Partnership—A syndication of investors (limited partners) who invest funds on a joint basis with a managing general partner. Investor's liability is limited to his/her original capital contribution.

Life Insurance Cash Values—The build-up of cash on an annual basis inside of a permanent (whole life, interest sensitive, or universal) life policy.

Money Market Account—A savings account that pays a money market (short-term securities) rate of interest.

INVESTMENT GLOSSARY (Continued)

Municipal Bond—A debt obligation issued by a state or local government agency. Income generated by such bonds is exempt from federal (and often state) income taxes.

Mutual Fund—An open end investment company. Ownership of shares in a portfolio of stocks and/or bonds which are professionally managed.

Preferred Stock—Noted for paying a fixed dividend. In the event of a corporate liquidation, holder of such stock would be paid before all common stock holders.

Real Estate Investment Trust (R.E.I.T.)—Ownership of shares in a portfolio of real estate properties or mortgage investments. At least 90% of the income passes through to the shareholders. Shares can be readily liquidated in the stock market.

U.S. Government Securities (Fund)—A professionally managed portfolio of debt obligations (bills, bonds, notes) issued or guaranteed by the U.S. government. Seeks high level of current income (usually 3-4 percentage points higher than money market rates) consistent with safety of principal. Similar to a mutual fund in structure.

U.S. Savings Bond—Guaranteed by the federal government. Purchased at a 50% discount from face value. Issued in face amounts from $50 to $10,000. No taxes to pay on accumulated interest until the bond is redeemed.

PRESCRIBING YOUR OWN INVESTMENT MEDICINE

It's time to prescribe your own investment medicine now that you have read over the Investment Section. Below, list the investments that you now have. On the right, circle the category into which each one falls (A - B - C - D) according to the Investment Chart on Page 73.

INVESTMENTS	CATEGORY
_____	A B C D
_____	A B C D
_____	A B C D
_____	A B C D
_____	A B C D

Does your Investment Portfolio match up with your objectives? Yes____ No____.
If not, prescribe what course of action might be needed.

INVESTMENTS	PRESCRIBED ACTION, IF ANY
_____	_____
_____	_____
_____	_____
_____	_____

AUTHOR'S NOTE

It might be appropriate to discuss and compare the above exercise with an experienced financial specialist who can help you fill your prescription.

SECTION IV

PLANNING FOR THE FUTURE

This section is devoted to three areas of financial planning that traditionally require long-term thinking and preparation; college funding, retirement planning, and estate planning.

COLLEGE FUNDING

If you have young children or plan to have children, the importance of long-term funding of college costs cannot be overstated. It may be appropriate for you to review the concept of dollar cost averaging on page 80 which provides for a long-term funding strategy. This concept emphasizes the importance of investing early and the compounding effect of money. You may also want to refer to the compound interest tables contained in Appendix B.

College costs have increased at a much higher rate than inflation for the past several years. Although the rate increase has slowed recently, college costs are still predicted to outpace inflation in the future.

By the year 2000, the average total cost for four years of college is expected to double. Financial aid for higher education, once a concern of low income families only, is now needed by almost everyone.

PLAN AHEAD FOR COLLEGE

COLLEGE FUNDING (continued)

Under present law, income earned in excess of $1,000 on (investment) funds held in the name of a child under age 14 will be taxed to the parents. The parents will pay the taxes on any excess income at their current income tax rate.

Example: Over the years John and Mary Smith have placed money in a savings account in the name of their 8 year old daughter, Tammy. Any interest earned on the account in excess of $1,000 must be reported by John and Mary on their tax return.

HOW TO AVOID THE PAYMENT OF TAXES IN THIS SITUATION:

There are currently four vehicles that would allow for the growth of the initial investment without incurring a tax. These are:

1. A Municipal Bond Fund—dividends can be reinvested and will compound tax free. Distributions are not taxed either.

2. A Single Premium Whole Life Contract—this is a single payment plan offered by an insurance company. Interest accumulates and compounds tax free. Under current legislation, accumulated interest may be withdrawn at a later date without tax consequences if the insurance contract was issued prior to June 20, 1988.

3. A Universal or Interest Sensitive Life Insurance Contract—such policies offer a cash value build-up which is not subject to taxation. Withdrawals may be made at a later date (by borrowing out the funds) without a tax consequence.

4. Series EE United States Savings Bonds—sold in denominations of $50 to $10,000. These bonds pay no current interest; they are purchased on a discount basis. Taxes on the annual increase in value can be postponed until the bonds mature or are redeemed (cashed-in).

It is suggested that you explore these options in greater detail with a financial planner. An investment program can be tailored to meet your specific needs.

INFORMATION SOURCES ON COLLEGE COSTS/FINANCIAL AID

Colleges can be an invaluable source of information. Contact the college(s) you are most interested in directly.

Also there are several helpful publications regarding college costs. Some of these sources include:

The Student Guide: Five Federal Financial Aid Programs (U.S. Government Printing Office, P.O. Box 37000, Washington, D.C. 20013). Describes all federal sources of financial aid in great detail and lists information sources for state aid for every state.

Applying for Financial Aid (American College Testing Program, P.O. Box 168, Iowa City, Iowa 52243).

The College Cost Book (College Entrance Examination Board, 45 Columbus Ave., New York, NY 10023). Available in most libraries and high school guidance counselor's offices.

Don't Miss Out, by Robert Leider (Octameron Press, P.O. Box 3437, Alexandria, VA 22302; $2.75). Contains needs-analysis forms and advice.

The College Handbook (Peterson Guides, Inc., 166 Bunn Drive, P.O. Box 2123, Princeton, NJ 08450; $9.95) Gives financial information on 1,700 U.S. colleges.

AUTHOR'S NOTE

You should discuss various funding plans with the colleges in which you are most interested. For example, you may be able to make a lump sum payment now (in the form of an annuity) and be guaranteed this sum of money will cover your child's college costs when he or she is old enough to begin college.

SYSTEMATIC INVESTING

WOULD YOU LIKE:

- an investment program for as little as $25 a month?

- a strategy designed to minimize risk of loss?

- a hedge against the uncertainties of the future?

- a method of systematically providing for future needs such as a college education for your children?

- a supplemental retirement plan?

THE NEXT PAGE MAY HELP CONVINCE YOU THAT A PLAN FOR SYSTEMATIC INVESTING IS A GOOD IDEA.

TIME ITSELF RATHER THAN TIMING IS A KEY ELEMENT OF INVESTMENT SUCCESS

THE ADVANTAGES OF SYSTEMATIC INVESTING

Systematic investing can pay great rewards over a period of time. To illustrate, let's take a look at a technique called "dollar cost averaging."

Dollar cost averaging is simply the investment of a certain sum of money (usually in the same security or mutual fund) at regular intervals over a long period of time. It is basically an application of *time diversification* that enables investors to acquire more shares when the price is down and fewer shares when the price is up. Over time this reduces the average cost of the investment.

This program is particularly well suited for investors:

1. Who have the ability to invest a specific amount of money on a regular basis.

2. Who tend to follow a general investment policy of buying and holding.

3. Who generally do not want to try to forecast general economic trends.

The bar graph shown below illustrates the power of systematic investing (or dollar cost averaging) and the benefits of compounding over time.

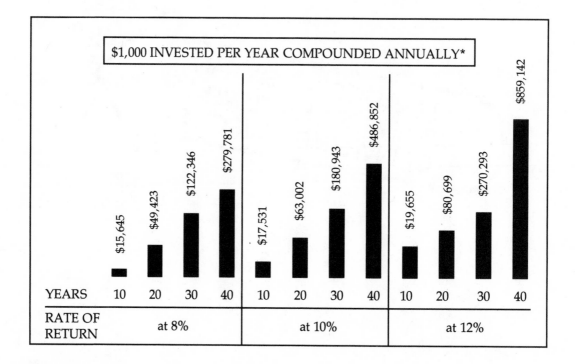

*Assumes investments at the beginning of each year.

RETIREMENT PLANNING

Today's 50 year olds can expect to live more than twenty years—approximately a third of their lives—in retirement.

Achieving financial security means accumulating a nest egg that will not only support you for two or three decades, but also resist the effects of inflation, taxation, or the possibility of failing health.

Successful retirement planning calls for astute investing, tax and estate planning, proper insurance management, and understanding social security and company sponsored pension benefits. Because it's your future, it's never too early to begin preparing for retirement.

There are five basic sources of retirement income:

1. Personal savings and investments

2. Employer sponsored retirement plans*

3. Retirement plans for small business owners and the self-employed*

4. The individual retirement account (IRA)*

5. Social Security

*For detailed information on qualified retirement plans and their tax treatment, refer to Section III, beginning on page 57.

Retirement also calls for planning in other areas of a person's life such as attitude, time-utilization, emotional and physical health, choice of housing, etc. For an outstanding book on retirement planning, send for *Comfort Zones: A Practical Guide for Retirement Planning* by Elwood Chapman using the special order form on page 126 of this book.

RETIREMENT PLANNING (continued)

The assumption is often made that an individual's financial needs decrease after retirement. Although often true, this reduction in needs can be overstated. There is an increasing tendency for retired persons to not only live longer but also to lead more active lives. A growing number of retirees are choosing to remain active in civic, social, and recreational activities and are not significantly decreasing their standard of living.

Proper planning for retirement is more important than ever due to increasing life expectancy and the risk of "outliving one's income". Also, despite the assurances of politicians, there is no guarantee that social security will be available—especially in its current form—when you retire.

If you determine your retirement objective—of a monthly income figure—falls short after you have completed the worksheet on page 86, one or more of the following variables will need to be changed or adjusted:

1. The amount you save or invest each year

2. The length of time until you retire

3. The annual growth rate on your investments

ARE YOU ADEQUATELY PREPARING FOR RETIREMENT?
THE TIME TO START PLANNING IS NOW!

DON'T LOSE CONTROL OF TIME

RETIREMENT PLANNING QUESTIONNAIRE

The questions listed below will help you to begin thinking about your future if you have not already begun to do so. Answer each honestly.

1. How many years until you expect to retire?

   _____

2. What monthly income (net of taxes) will allow you to live comfortably?

   _____

3. Have you checked with the Social Security Administration to verify your contributions and monthly benefit?

   _____

4. Does your company have a pension plan? If so, record the amount of your monthly income at retirement.

   _____

5. Are you presently contributing the maximum amount allowable to a company sponsored retirement program? If so, how much?

   _____

6. If self-employed, are you contributing to a Keogh (pension/profit sharing plan)? If so, how much?

   _____

7. Have you been making annual contributions to an IRA?

   _____

8. If you are an employee of a non-profit organization or a school district, are you contributing to a tax sheltered annuity (TSA)?

   _____

9. What amount of income (after taxes) will your investments provide on a monthly basis?

   _____

10. Will you work part-time after retirement?

   _____

Now that you are in a ''retirement'' frame of mind, complete the exercise on the next page.

THE GOLDEN YEARS—WILL THEY GLITTER?

RETIREMENT GOALS

List those things you would like for a satisfying and fulfilling retirement. Consider where you want to live and what you want to do. Include travel and recreation in your plans. Don't worry about whether or not you can afford it now, just record what you really want. Use more paper if necessary.

_____
_____
_____
_____
_____
_____
_____
_____

Monthly Income And Expenses Worksheet

It's important to know your monthly financial needs both now and when you retire. You'll learn this by listing your average monthly income and expenses*. The difference between what you now earn and what you spend is important, because it represents the amount you will need to invest in your future. The table on page 85 will help you determine your income needs and expenses at retirement based on the inflation rate you select.

MONTHLY INCOME	NOW*	RETIREMENT
Salary (including spouse's)	$_____	$_____
Commissions, Bonuses, Tips	_____	_____
Interest, Dividends	_____	_____
Social Security	_____	_____
Pensions, Annuities, Trusts	_____	_____
Other	_____	_____
TOTAL INCOME (A)	$_____	$_____

MONTHLY EXPENSES	NOW*	RETIREMENT
Housing (mortgage payments/rent)	$_____	$_____
Maintenance & Repairs	_____	_____
Utilities	_____	_____
Loan payments (car, personal)	_____	_____
Food	_____	_____
Clothing	_____	_____
Transportation	_____	_____
Medical (health) expenses	_____	_____
Insurance premiums	_____	_____
Recreation/travel	_____	_____
Charitable contributions	_____	_____
Taxes—property, income	_____	_____
Other	_____	_____
TOTAL EXPENSES (B)	$_____	$_____
A − B = SURPLUS (OR DEFICIT)	$_____	$_____

*Your current figures can be obtained from the Income (or Cash Flow) Statement that you previously completed on page 19.

INFLATION TABLE

Additional Income
(in dollars)
Needed At Retirement,
With Various Inflation Rates

Years Until Retirement	5%	8%	10%	12%	15%
10	1.63	2.16	2.59	3.11	4.05
11	1.71	2.33	2.85	3.48	4.65
12	1.80	2.52	3.14	3.90	5.35
13	1.89	2.72	3.45	4.36	6.15
14	1.98	2.94	3.80	4.89	7.08
15	2.08	3.17	4.18	5.47	8.14
16	2.18	3.43	4.60	6.13	9.36
17	2.29	3.70	5.05	6.87	10.77
18	2.41	4.00	5.56	7.69	12.38
19	2.53	4.32	6.12	8.61	14.23
20	2.65	4.66	6.73	9.65	16.37
21	2.79	5.03	7.40	10.80	18.82
22	2.93	5.44	8.14	12.10	21.64
23	3.07	5.87	8.95	13.55	24.89
24	3.23	6.34	9.85	15.18	28.63
25	3.39	6.85	10.83	17.00	32.92
26	3.56	7.40	11.92	19.04	37.86
27	3.73	7.99	13.11	21.32	43.54
28	3.92	8.63	14.42	23.88	50.07
29	4.12	9.32	15.86	26.75	57.58
30	4.32	10.06	17.45	29.96	66.22

HOW TO USE TABLE: Say, for example, that John and Mary are currently living on $2,000 a month. John plans to retire in 15 years. Assuming an annual inflation rate of 5% over that period of time, what amount would be needed at retirement to maintain their current standard of living.

To find the answer, come down the 5% inflation rate to the 15th year. The figure is 2.08. Multiply the monthly income of $2,000 by 2.08. This figure of $4,160 ($2,000 × 2.08) is the amount of income needed at retirement to maintain their current standard of living.

RETIREMENT PLANNING EXERCISE

What have you learned? Will your income at retirement be sufficient to meet your expenditures? If not, what adjustments can you begin to make to correct the situation? In the space below, list those action items which will be necessary to meet your retirement objectives. For example, save more each month, reduce outstanding debt, plan to work 10 hours per week (even when officially retired), cut back on your retirement expectations, delay the age of your retirement, etc.

_____

_____

_____

_____

_____

_____

_____

_____

_____

_____

_____

_____

_____

_____

SOCIAL SECURITY AND MEDICARE

Questions on Social Security

Q. How old must I be to qualify for Social Security?

A. You must be at least sixty-two.

Q. When and where should I file for Social Security benefits?

A. Three months before you plan to retire. Apply at your local Social Security Administration office.

Q. Does the Social Security Administration require any special papers when I file?

A. Yes. Bring your Social Security card, a copy of your birth or baptismal certificate, and a copy of your last withholding income tax statement or Federal income tax return.

Q. How do I qualify for benefits?

A. You receive credit for a certain amount of work. Work credits are figured in "quarters of coverage". You get one quarter of coverage if your wages come to at least $370 in a quarter of a year. To be "fully insured"—that is, to be guaranteed full retirement benefits—you need 33 quarters if you reach 62 in 1984, 34 quarters if you reach age 62 in 1985. The maximum requirement of 40 quarters (10 years) will be reached in 1991.

Q. How much will I get?

A. This varies from person to person, depending on individual factors (such as the number of years you worked, your average yearly earnings, your age at retirement, etc.). Your Social Security office will figure it out for you after you apply. Currently, the maximum monthly benefit for a retired worker at age 65 is over $700.

SOCIAL SECURITY & MEDICARE (continued)

Q. How much can I earn and still get my full Social Security retirement check?

A. The 1989 limits on annual earnings are $6,480.00 for those between the ages of 62 and 65 and $8, 880.00 for those in the age group 65 to 70. There is no limit on the amount an individual can earn who is age 70 or older.

Social Security checks will be reduced by $1.00 in benefits for each $2.00 earned over the maximum allowed.

Unearned income such as interest, stock dividends, and income from rental property will not affect Social Security payments.

Medicare Health Insurance Information

Medicare is a federal health insurance program for people age 65 and older. It also covers some people under 65 who are disabled. You must enroll to receive Medicare coverage. The initial enrollment period for medicare begins 3 months before you reach age 65 and lasts for 7 months. You must apply at your local Social Security Administration office during the 7 month period in order to receive medicare coverage when you first become eligible.

Medicare has two parts: (A) Hospital Insurance and (B) Medical Insurance. The basic hospital insurance plan will pay for most of the costs related to hospitalization as well as certain related care when you leave the hospital. The medical insurance plan pays for a large part of your doctor bills plus other medical expenses not covered by the basic hospital insurance plan.

There is no monthly cost to you for Hospital Insurance, but you must pay a monthly premium for Medical Insurance which is normally deducted from your social security check.

For an excellent book on Social Security & Medicare—order *The Complete & Easy Guide to Social Security & Medicare*. This practical, inexpensive worktext is updated each year. Order using the special form on page 126.

MEDICARE SUPPLEMENTAL PREMIUM

All taxpayers 65 and over, who are eligible for Social Security benefits must pay an annual Supplemental Medicare Premium. This must be reported and paid with the 1989 Federal Income Tax Return.

This Supplemental Premium is based on your tax liability and in 1989 will be *$22.50 for EVERY $150.00 in tax owed.* The premium doubles in the case of a joint return where both spouses are eligible for Medicare coverage. For a couple with a tax bill of $1,800 in 1989, the additional Medicare Premium would be $270.00 times 2 or $540.00. ($1,800/$150 = 12 × $22.50 = $270.00 × 2 individuals filing jointly.)

These supplemental premiums escalate each year through 1993 and the figures for the increased amount are shown below. Maximum premiums per taxpayer for each period are also shown.

Year	Rate Per $150 Tax Liability	Maximum Premium -Single-	Maximum Premium -Joint-
1989	$22.50	$ 800.00	$1,600.00
1990	37.50	850.00	1,700.00
1991	39.00	900.00	1,800.00
1992	40.50	950.00	1,900.00
1993	42.00	1,050.00	2,100.00

AUTHOR'S NOTE

The Catastrophic Coverage Act translates to an increased tax bill for the elderly. For this reason, older investors for whom investments provide a large source of income, should consider repositioning their portfolios so that tax-free income plays a larger role. Some of the more effective strategies would be to invest in a combination of tax-free Money Market Funds, tax-free Municipal Bonds, and immediate annuities.

For information on assistance and services for the elderly, see Appendix C on page 121.

ESTATE PLANNING

Estate planning, at its simplest, involves the preservation and distribution of wealth, either before or after death.

Proper estate planning can help to:

1. alleviate administrative court costs

2. provide for orderly distribution of assets without delay

3. minimize legal fees and estate taxes

Despite the necessity for, and advantage of, early planning to divide one's estate, most people are reluctant to deal with the subject. A financial planner can review your estate situation and then direct you to an attorney who specializes in this particular field of law. A financial planner can "nudge" you to do what you know should be done.

> Once again, the objective is to have you examine and diagnose your needs in this very critical area.

ESTATE PLANNING IS A MUST

PERSONAL ESTATE PLAN ANALYSIS

This short exercise will help you think about your estate and determine what provisions may be needed to preserve your wealth for the benefit of your survivors.

	Yes	No	I Don't Know
Do I have a will?	_____	_____	_____
Has my will been revised during the last three years to adjust for any significant changes in my personal/financial situation or estate tax legislation?	_____	_____	_____
Do I understand the different tax ramifications of holding title to my assets—i.e., joint tenancy vs. community property.	_____	_____	_____
Have I considered any special problems my survivors might have? (example: handicaps, personalities, abilities)	_____	_____	_____
Are there any special tax planning provisions (such as a trust) in my estate plan?	_____	_____	_____
Will my estate provide enough liquidity to meet immediate family needs and pay all outstanding debts?	_____	_____	_____
Do my heirs/executor know where to locate my important papers and documents?*	_____	_____	_____
Upon my death, will my children's interests be protected in the event my spouse remarries?	_____	_____	_____
Have I recently reviewed the beneficiary designation of my life insurance policies, IRAs and company retirement plans to determine if any changes might be appropriate?	_____	_____	_____

If you have *not* answered yes to at least five of the questions, it indicates a lack of attention to this area of your financial affairs. Meeting with a financial planner or estate planning attorney would be advisable.

———————

*Before answering, please refer to Appendix A regarding the location of your personal financial records. If you have not collected this information, now would be an excellent time to do so using the forms provided.

ESTATE PLANNING (continued)

WHY A WILL IS IMPORTANT

Several reasons. First, Uncle Sam gets more if you die intestate (without a will). Also, there are delays, higher court costs, and the involvement of state appointed administrators (strangers) to settle your personal affairs if you do not have a will.

WHAT A WILL CAN DO

If you die testate (with a will), your assets will be distributed according to the terms of the will. Your personal wishes and instructions will be carried out.

ADDITIONAL METHODS OF TRANSFERRING ASSETS TO AN HEIR:

1. Gift—i.e., giving property away outright.

2. Title—i.e., joint tenancy with the right of survivorship (JT/WROS). For example: property titled John Doe and Mary Doe as Joint Tenants will pass to the survivor of these two regardless of what the will might state.

3. Contract—i.e., naming someone as the beneficiary in a life insurance policy. At the time of death of the insured, the named beneficiary will receive the designated amount directly from the insurance company free of income taxes.

4. Trust*—a separate legal entity created for (1) tax planning or estate tax reduction, (2) eliminating probate costs and delays, (3) family planning— determining when and how much to distribute.

   All assets transferred by you to the trust will be distributed according to your written instructions contained within the trust document.

The above methods should be thoughtfully coordinated (with the help of an estate planning attorney) to maximize the financial benefits to those for whom you wish to provide. Your estate plan should be reviewed every two or three years to make adjustments for changes in tax laws or your personal/financial situation.

*See the next page for a discussion of a living trust.

THE LIVING TRUST
A VERSATILE ESTATE PLANNING TOOL

WHAT IT IS

An arrangement whereby you (as Trustor) transfer legal ownership of your property to yourself as Trustee. For example: John and Mary Thomas would transfer title to their house from ''John and Mary Thomas as joint tenants'' to ''John and Mary Thomas, Trustees of the Thomas Family Trust.''

HOW TO ESTABLISH

The trust document must be prepared by an attorney. It is a flexible arrangement which costs you, as Trustee, virtually nothing to administer during your lifetime. The living trust (also known as an Inter Vivos Trust) may be amended or revoked (terminated) while you, and your spouse, if married are alive. When either spouse dies, the trust document becomes irrevocable.

BENEFITS*

- It provides privacy—the trust document does not become a part of the public record.

- It avoids probate and unnecessary delays in settling your estate.

- It can eliminate the payment of income taxes on highly appreciated property.

- It can be structured to provide professional management of the assets for the surviving spouse, if he/she has little investment or business experience.

- It provides for a conservatorship in the event of physical or mental incapacitation.

- It can save your estate money by reducing estate taxes at the second death.

- It reduces chances of having your estate contested by a disgruntled heir. The establishment of a trust shows clear intent on your part.

- Finally, it is a valuable planning tool to benefit those with moderate-size estates to very large estates.

The above is one major type of trust. Be aware there are many different types of trusts available to meet your specific objectives. Consult an estate planning specialist for specific trust(s) that may be appropriate for you.

---

*The total number of benefits will vary according to your particular circumstances.

ESTATE PLANNING GLOSSARY

Beneficiary a person named to receive the income or property from a trust or life insurance policy.

Community Property property that either or both spouses acquire during marriage. Each spouse has an undivided half interest in their community property. Upon death, each spouse can dispose of *only* his or her half of the community property by will. This form of property ownership is limited to a few states.

Estate the total amount of assets and liabilities belonging to a person at the time of his/her death.

Executor/ Executrix the personal representative appointed in a will to settle an estate. It can be either a person or a corporate entity such as a bank or trust company.

Guardian/ Conservator a person appointed by the court to take care of the needs of a minor, incapacitated or incompetent person (the ward). The guardian's duty to care for the ward's needs continues until the ward reaches the age of majority, or once again, becomes competent.

Heir one receiving a person's property (inheritance) either by will or law.

Joint Tenancy the co-ownership of property by two or more persons related or unrelated. Upon death of a co-owner, the surviving owner(s) automatically receive(s) the deceased's share. No probate is involved.

Living Will an expression of an individual's wish that when faced with imminent death, sophisticated, life-sustaining medical technology should not be used to prolong life. This declaration should be kept separate from a person's legal will.

Probate the process by which a court determines legal title to property following a death. Probate can be costly and time consuming.

Trust an arrangement in which one party (Trustee) holds legal title to property for the benefit of another (Beneficiary). Often used to avoid probate and reduce estate taxes.

Will a validly executed document that disposes of an individual's property and other owned interests when he/she dies.

PLANNED GIVING ARRANGEMENTS

CHARITY BEGINS AT HOME

How would you like to:

1. Generate an income tax deduction.

2. Increase and diversify your income.

3. Avoid the payment of a capital gains tax on highly appreciated/low yielding assets (typically stocks or real estate).

4. Eliminate asset management problems.

5. Reduce estate taxes.

6. Avoid probate costs.

7. Assist your favorite charity.

These benefits can be obtained by contributing a currently owned asset to a charitable organization.

PLANNED GIVING EXAMPLE

Let's take the example of Mr. and Mrs. Johnson to illustrate how a charitable contribution works.

Facts

Presently, the Johnsons own a $100,000 stock portfolio generating total dividends of $1,500 a year. The original value of the stock portfolio was $50,000.

The Johnsons would like to increase their income but are reluctant to sell the securities because of the estimated capital gains tax ($50,000 × 28% federal tax bracket = $14,000 in taxes).

Action To Take

Donate the stocks to their favorite charity using a vehicle called a Charitable Remainder Trust (sometimes also called a Wealth Accumulation Trust).

The charity sells the stock. The proceeds ($100,000) are invested to generate an 8% yield or $8,000 per year. The Johnsons will receive this income for as long as either one is alive. Upon the death of the last survivor, the charity receives the $100,000. The Johnsons also receive the initial tax write-off* of $40,000. In a 28% bracket, the immediate tax savings would be $11,200.

*The tax write-off will vary according to the donor's age.

PLANNED GIVING EXAMPLE (continued)

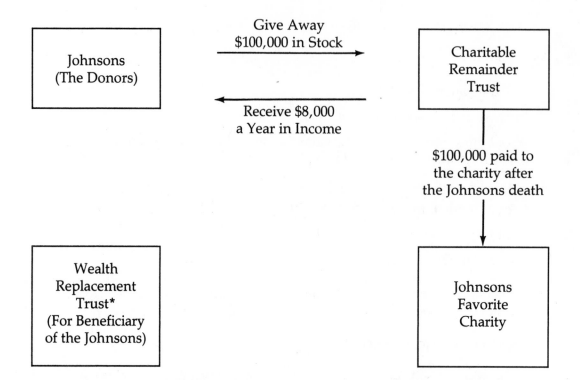

*The Wealth Replacement Trust is, in effect, an irrevocable life insurance trust. The trust, with premium payments provided by the Johnsons, purchases a life insurance contract on the lives of the Johnsons. The heirs of the Johnsons would receive the life insurance proceeds free of probate costs and income taxes.

BENEFITS WITH CHARITABLE TRUST IN PLACE

Current Income Tax Saved	$11,200
Annual Cash Flow Increased by	6,500
Capital Gains Tax Avoided	14,000

AUTHOR'S NOTE

The area of charitable giving is very personal and can be quite complex and sophisticated. For these reasons, it is advisable to consult with professional advisors. You may want to start by contacting your favorite charity.

SECTION V

CASE STUDIES

AUTHOR'S NOTES

The purpose of the following four case studies (client situations) is to let you practice your working knowledge of the terms, concepts and principles covered in this book. You can practice prescribing specific courses of action. There are no absolutely correct answers.

Everyone's situation should be reviewed annually to adjust for significant changes in personal or financial circumstances or tax laws. This annual review stresses the importance of monitoring, which is essential to the financial planning process.

The road to success is paved with good intentions, sound investments *and* proper planning.

CASE STUDY NO. 1

MAXIMIZING INVESTMENT RETURNS

Personal Information

Tom Wilton, age 51
Senior engineer with an aerospace firm
Annual income $75,000
Mary Wilton, age 48
Housewife
Two grown children
Have lived in same home for 21 years
Both have a moderate tolerance for risk

Financial Information

$37,500—in various savings and money market accounts; average yield of 5%.

$12,000 in several low yielding stocks (3.5%).

A 20 year old $10,000 insurance contract containing $5,000 in cash values; annual cash value build-up is 4.5%.

A $100,000 company sponsored group term insurance policy.

$650 in monthly surplus which is added to savings.

Goals and Objectives

Generate a higher yield on investments but take only moderate risk to do so.

Maintain an emergency fund of at least $10,000.

YOUR RECOMMENDATIONS

-
-
-

Compare your recommendations with the author's recommendations on the facing page.

Author's Suggested Recommendations

Observations

The Wiltons presently have no capital growth potential and little protection from taxation.

Recommendations

Surrender the life insurance policy for the $5,000 in cash values. Sell the low yielding stocks. Invest the total proceeds ($17,000) in a Single Premium Deferred Annuity Contract.

Invest $10,000 from current savings/money market accounts ($37,500) in a U.S. Government Securities fund. Income is taxable but yields are usually 3-4 percentage points higher than money market accounts.

Invest $5,000 from current savings/money market accounts ($37,500) into each of three balanced (a combination of growth and income) mutual funds. Income and gains are subject to ordinary income taxation.

Add $150 per month from the $650 monthly surplus available in each balanced mutual fund. This systematic approach to investing is a form of dollar cost averaging. The remaining $200 monthly surplus should be added to a tax-free money market account.

Put half of remaining current savings/money market accounts ($6,250) into a tax-free money market fund in order to generate a higher net (after tax) return. Leave remaining half of reserves ($6,250) in the savings account.

Results

The annuity contract will provide a higher net yield than either the life insurance cash values or the stocks. Interest will accumulate and compound tax free and can be earmarked to supplement retirement income.

The U.S. Government Securities will generate a higher return with only moderate risk.

The monthly mutual fund investment program represents a conservative approach to long-term investing (dollar cost averaging). The growth potential of the funds represents a hedge against inflation.

CASE STUDY NO. 2

HELPING THE SINGLE PARENT SURVIVE

Personal Information

Pamela Atkins, age 39
Office Administrator for a small software firm that does not have a retirement
  plan in force
Annual salary $24,000
Recently divorced—lives with 15 yr. old daughter, Diane
Ex-husband provides $700 per month in child support. He also maintains a
  $50,000 life insurance policy naming Pam as the beneficiary.

Financial Information

Pamela and Diane currently live in an apartment renting for $850 per month.

When former residence (owned with ex-husband) is sold, Pamela will receive
$38,000 in cash (after taxes).

Has $2,500 in savings, $5,000 in credit card debt (18% annual interest rate);
maximum monthly payments on credit cards are $250.

Pamela recently received an inheritance of $17,000 from her father's estate which
she placed in a 90 day Certificate of Deposit.

Pamela has never attempted to budget her income or expenses.

Goals and Objectives

Feel comfortable and in control of current financial situation.

Purchase a $90,000 condominum.

Build a reserve for the future (retirement fund).

YOUR RECOMMENDATIONS

-
-
-

Compare your recommendations with the author's recommendations on the
facing page.

Author's Suggested Recommendations

Observations

Short term debt (credit cards) has a negative impact on monthly cash flow.

Must control finances through diligent use of a budget (income and expense forecasting).

Recommendations

Develop a monthly Income (or cash flow) Statement and Create a monthly Budget. Monitor both on a regular basis. Attempt to develop a monthly surplus to add to the savings account.

Once an amount equal to three months fixed living expenses (estimated at $5,000) has been reached in the savings account, use the cash surplus to fund a monthly investment program (dollar cost averaging) in a growth mutual fund or a real estate investment trust (R.E.I.T.).

Use $5,000 of the inheritance money to pay off *all* credit card debt (18% interest) when the CD matures in 90 days.

Use proceeds from sale of previous home and $2,000 of the inheritance funds to place $40,000 on a $90,000 condominium. Monthly payments (estimated at $800 including property taxes) consist largely of tax deductible interest, thereby generating a tax savings of $200 per month. The remainder of the inheritance ($10,000) can be used to upgrade and furnish the condominium.

Of the $200 per month in tax savings, $166 can be used to invest in an IRA which will generate another $2,000 tax deduction for the year.

Results

Creation of the Income Statement and Budget will help Pam monitor her cash flow on a more consistent basis and give her a feeling of being in better control of her finances.

Elimination of credit card debt and use of the monthly surplus for savings (initially) and then investing, will help build financial security for the future.

Purchase of a condominum will create a tax write-off through interest and property tax deductions. The IRA will also create a tax write-off while building a retirement fund for the future.

CASE STUDY NO. 3

ADDING GLITTER TO THE GOLDEN YEARS

Personal Information

Harold Smith, age 64
Senior Manager for a public utilities company
Annual salary $57,000
Betty Smith, age 57
Housewife. Has no interest in financial matters. Harold has always managed their money.
Harold will retire in one year at age 65
Neither has a will at the present time
Have 4 grown children, all of whom are married
Own a four unit apartment building

Financial Information

Estimated gross monthly income needed at retirement—$3,000

Projected sources of monthly retirement income:

company pension plan	$1,700
social security	$ 800
rental income (fourplex)	$ 400
Total	$2,900

Estimated vested benefits from company salary savings program at age 65 is $125,000. An estimate of the annual income that can be generated from this source has *not* been included in the projected sources of monthly retirement income.

$20,000 in a Certificate of Deposit maturing in one year.

Has contributed to an IRA for the past five years. All funds are currently in the company credit union (total value of $15,000).

Goals and Objectives

Maximize income to provide for a comfortable retirement.

At retirement, stay ahead of inflation without depleting investment principal.

Simplify the tracking and administration of all investments at retirement.

Provide for the efficient and orderly disposition of assets in the event of either spouse's death.

YOUR RECOMMENDATIONS

-
-
-

Compare your recommendations with the author's recommendations on the facing page.

Author's Suggested Recommendations

Observations

The Smiths live within their means and should enjoy a comfortable retirement.

Recommendations

When the $20,000 Certificate of Deposit matures, place the $10,000 into an insured Money Market Account to serve as an emergency fund. Place the remaining $10,000 in a single premium deferred annuity contract.

Establish a self-directed trust and transfer the existing IRA accounts (currently in the company credit union) into this account. Invest one half of the money in a U.S. Government Securities fund and the other half in a Single Premium Tax Deferred Annuity. Selection of a joint and last survivor annuity option will guarantee a monthly income as long as either spouse is alive.

At retirement, rollover the vested company retirement funds ($125,000) into the self-directed trust and place the funds into income-oriented investments. Harold may make withdrawals from this account at any time to supplement his monthly retirement income. There are no income taxes to pay on the funds in the self-directed trust until withdrawn.

See an estate planning attorney to draft an estate plan designed to meet the needs of both Harold and Betty. Placing their assets in an inter vivos (living) trust with a provision for professional management will be of great benefit to Betty if Harold predeceases her.

Results

The retirement funds placed in the self-directed trust will accumulate and compound tax free. Any additional monthly income needed may be withdrawn from the trust account (and will be subject to ordinary income taxation).

The establishment of a $10,000 money market account will provide the Smiths with an emergency source of funds equal to approximately three times their fixed living expenses ($3,000 × 3 mos. = $9,000).

The interest on the annuity contract is taxed only if withdrawn. A good tax deferral investment.

Drafting an estate plan will provide for the orderly disposition of their assets and provide Betty with the protection and investment advice that she needs.

CASE STUDY NO. 4

PROVIDING FOR THE FUTURE

Personal Information

Ron Woodman, age 45
Sales representative for a manufacturing firm
Annual salary $75,000
Janice Woodman, age 40
Housewife.
Have two children, ages 15 and 12

Financial Information

Annual amount available for investing or savings—$4,500

Ron is currently contributing 3% (6% is allowable) to his company's 401(k) plan

A college fund has been established for the children by the grandparents

Have stocks in various Mutual Funds valued at $25,000

Have $10,000 in a bank passbook account

Goals and Objectives

Provide greater insurance protection for Janice and the children

Earmark funds for college expenses

Build a reserve to supplement future retirement income

YOUR RECOMMENDATIONS

-
-
-

Compare your recommendations with the author's recommendations on the facing page.

Author's Suggested Recommendations

Observations

The Woodmans are very disciplined financially as evidenced by their annual surplus of $4,500.

Contributions made by the grandparents will greatly help to reduce college costs.

Recommendations

Use $2,250 of the annual surplus to purchase a $160,000 insurance policy with a seven year vanishing premium. The estimated cash value at 65 would be $36,153.

Use the balance of the disposable income ($2,250) to increase Ron's contributions to his 401(k) contribution to a maximum of 6% of salary. All earnings on his contributions will accumulate tax free until withdrawn at retirement.

Earmark stocks and mutual funds to supplement future college expenses.

Transfer the funds in the bank passbook account to an insured Money Market Account.

Results

The insurance policy will provide a tax free death benefit and a cash value of $36,153 at age 65. Ron could, at that time, borrow out of the contract on a tax free basis $3,500 per month (for more than 20 years) to supplement his retirement income.

Using the securities to supplement college costs will avoid the necessity to use current income which can then go into the programs (the insurance contract and the 401(k) contributions) which will provide greater income at retirement.

The insured Money Market Account will provide a higher yield than the passbook account with commensurate safety.

You have spent a considerable amount of time gathering personal and financial data and evaluating it to determine your overall strengths, weaknesses and needs. Most of your efforts thus far have been in Step 1 (examine) and Step 2 (diagnose) of the financial planning process. To a lesser degree, you have been involved in Step 3 (prescribe) and Step 4 (monitor).

The self-scoring fitness exam on page 111 will test your understanding of the basic concepts discussed in this book. Your comprehension of these concepts combined with the evaluation of your current financial position may lead you to the conclusion that the services of a financial advisor would be beneficial. If you feel this is the case, the information on how to select a financial planner will be helpful to you.

SECTION VI

MONITOR
THE RESULTS

THE FINANCIAL FITNESS EXAM

The following exam will help you determine your basic understanding of the material presented in this book.

1.	Personal financial planning goals should be general in nature.	T	F
2.	Life insurance payments to a named beneficiary are taxable as ordinary income.	T	F
3.	A living (inter vivos) trust will benefit those with modest estates as well as those with very large estates.	T	F
4.	An income (or cash flow) statement lists all of your assets and liabilities.	T	F
5.	Current tax law allows for the deduction of state and local income taxes and real estate (property) taxes against ordinary income.	T	F
6.	Keeping secret the whereabouts of personal papers will provide for greater family security.	T	F
7.	Both municipal and corporate bonds generate tax free income.	T	F
8.	The income earned on an IRA must be reported as taxable income each year.	T	F
9.	School district or non-profit organization employees may contribute to a tax sheltered annuity (TSA).	T	F
10.	Married people usually die intestate.	T	F
11.	The longer the maturity date, the greater the appreciation on a bank Certificate of Deposit.	T	F
12.	Diversification is a sound defensive strategy towards investing.	T	F
13.	Dollar cost averaging is well suited for short term needs such as your next vacation.	T	F
14.	Anyone over age 30 could benefit from long term planning.	T	F
15.	Mortgage interest deductions on first and second homes are limited to the sum total of the price you originally paid for the house plus the cost of home (capital) improvements.	T	F
16.	The interest on consumer debt (such as credit cards) will continue to be a viable tax deductible item.	T	F
17.	There are insurance products that generate tax free income.	T	F
18.	Bankruptcy is a form of financial risk.	T	F
19.	A young married couple with a small income should invest discretionary funds in municipal bonds.	T	F
20.	A budget is used to forecast income and expenses.	T	F

Grading Key	
Number correct	
16-20	You're on the way to ''financial fitness''
10-15	It's time to schedule a routine check-up. Review the sections you found most difficult.
Less than 10	Take two aspirin, read the book again, and call a financial planner in the morning!

ANSWERS TO THE EXAM

1. F. Goals should be specific—use dollar figures and dates.

2. F. Proceeds to a named beneficiary are received income tax free.

3. T. A living (inter vivos) trust is a versatile estate planning tool which offers both tax and non tax benefits.

4. F. A *balance sheet* lists your assets and liabilities. The *income statement* lists your income and expenses.

5. T. These provisions remain unaffected by the 1986 Tax Reform Act.

6. F. Key advisors, family members and your executor/executrix should know the location of all important financial information.

7. F. Only a municipal bond will generate tax free income.

8. F. Income accumulates and compounds tax free. Only when funds are withdrawn are they subject to taxation.

9. T.

10. F. The term "intestate" means to die without a will.

11. F. The original deposit does not appreciate in value. It generates taxable income.

12. T.

13. F. It is better suited to long term needs such as college funding or retirement.

14. T. It's never too early to prepare for the future.

15. T. However, this sum may be exceeded if you borrow against your home for qualified educational or medical expenses.

16. F. As a deduction it will be completely phased out by 1991.

17. T. It is possible to borrow the accumulated cash values in a Whole Life or Universal Life Contract and thereby avoid paying income taxes.

18. T.

19. F. Growth of capital is more important than tax exempt income in a low tax bracket.

20. T. A budget looks at your future plan for earning and spending money.

HOW TO CHOOSE A FINANCIAL PLANNER

AUTHOR'S NOTE

Many financial planners do not charge for the initial one hour consultation. The objective of this initial meeting is to learn about each other. Bring information to your first meeting such as a balance sheet, last year's tax return, estate plan documents, insurance policies and retirement plan benefits. Be prepared to discuss your situation in specific terms.

You and the planner should be compatible. This is often determined by his/her investment philosophy as compared to your own. Also you should feel a high level of trust (just as with your personal physician). You should feel confident and comfortable with your planner. The following checklist should help you to evaluate and select a financial planning professional:

QUESTIONS TO ASK AND POINTS TO CONSIDER:

1. Ask to see a sample of the planner's work, such as an investment analysis or financial plan. The planner should provide concrete evidence of his/her competence and ability to deal with a vast array of financial situations.

2. Ask what type of clientele the planner works with. It is common for planners to work within particular professional groups, income levels and/or age groups.

3. Request a disclosure statement that provides details of the planner's education, number of years experience, background and also that of key staff members. The size of the firm is not as important as the qualifications of the planner.

4. Ask the planner to provide the names of clients who you may contact regarding the quality of service rendered.

5. Ask to see credentials. Industry credentials such as Certified Financial Planner (CFP) and membership in the Registry of Financial Planning Practitioners (established by the IAFP) indicate a commitment to excellence. Either of these credentials identify practitioners with the education, experience and ethics considered necessary to perform their services professionally.

   To become a CFP, an individual must pass a six part curriculum and have a minimum of three years of full-time experience of direct client contact.

   The standards for the Registry of Financial Planning Practitioners have been established by the IAFP and help the public identify financial planning practitioners who meet the standards essential to the practice of total financial planning. To be a Registry member, an individual must hold certain approved designations, certifications, or degrees and have a minimum of three years experience practicing total financial planning.

6. Inquire if the planner is a member in good standing of the International Association for Financial Planning (IAFP) and the Institute of Certified Financial Planners (ICFP).

   IAFP—has a broad based membership that comes from many related disciplines: financial planners, accountants, attorneys, bankers, trust officers, representatives of the insurance, real estate and securities field, and suppliers of various financial products and services.

   ICFP—only Certified Financial Planners can be members.

7. Discuss the planner's method of compensation, which may be:

   - Fees—Either an hourly rate or a flat charge for a specific period of time (such as one year). Fees are usually determined on a case-by-case basis.

   - Commissions—Generated from investment products placed through the planner.

   - Fees and Commissions—Those planners who are Registered Investment Advisors (RIA) may charge a fee as well as receive commissions.

8. Ask questions. Learn as much as you can about the planner. This can initially be accomplished both by phone and during the introductory meeting.

HOW TO CONTACT A FINANCIAL ADVISOR

- Through a friend or associate currently working with an advisor who is satisfied with the results.

- Through a national organization such as those listed below, who will provide referrals in your area:

ICFP—Institute of Certified Financial Planners, Two Denver Highlands, 10065 E. Harvard Ave., Ste. 320, Denver, CO 80231
(303) 751-7600

IAFP—International Association for Financial Planning, Two Concourse Parkway, Ste. 800, Atlanta, GA 30328
(404) 395-1605

Registry of Financial Planning Practitioners, Two Concourse Parkway, Ste. 800, Atlanta, GA 30328
(404) 395-1605

- Via free public seminars. Many financial planners, accountants, and attorneys conduct informational seminars that could be of interest to you. Consult your local newspaper for announcements.

- Through the yellow pages. (Sometimes the best planners don't advertise their services.)

- Through courses offered by your local community college or adult education program.

AUTHOR'S NOTE

In addition to the services offered by independent financial planners, you may wish to explore the services offered by the financial planning departments of various banks, insurance companies, and stock brokerage firms. In all cases, the same questions should be asked.

PERSONAL ACTION SCHEDULE

The personal action schedule (below) is designed to help you establish priorities (and completion dates) for those things you regard as most important. Items on the schedule serve only as a guide to stimulate your thinking. Feel free to add, change, or eliminate any of them to suit your particular needs.

ITEM		DATE COMPLETED
ESTABLISH	a specific set of financial goals	_____
DEVELOP	a balance sheet and income statement	_____
ANALYZE	your current financial situation in light of your goals	_____
EVALUATE	each of your investments in terms of income, growth and tax advantages relative to your goals	_____
SELECT	investments and strategies that will improve your overall financial fitness	_____
REVIEW	your estate plan and insurance coverage—life, health, disability, property and casualty	_____

OTHER ACTION ITEMS:

_____   _____

_____   _____

_____   _____

_____   _____

_____   _____

Completion of the personal action schedule will clarify what you wish to accomplish and give you a sense of direction.

APPENDIX A

RECORD OF IMPORTANT FINANCIAL INFORMATION

Checking account (No. _____)   (No. _____)

Located at: _____   _____

                  _____   _____

Savings account   (No. _____)   (No. _____)

Located at: _____   _____

                  _____   _____

Other—(Credit Union, Certificate of Deposit, etc.)

                  (No. _____)   (No. _____)

Located at: _____   _____

                  _____   _____

                  _____   _____

Key Advisors:	*Name*	*Addresses*	*Telephone*
Attorney	_____	_____	_____
Accountant	_____	_____	_____
Financial Planner	_____	_____	_____
Banker	_____	_____	_____
Insurance Agent	_____	_____	_____
Stock Broker	_____	_____	_____
Other	_____	_____	_____
Other	_____	_____	_____

(This page may be reproduced without further permission)   (over)

Safety Deposit Box (SDB) No. _____

Located at: _____

Keys to box are located at: _____

Location of important documents and papers: Check one

	Home	Office	Safety Deposit Box
Wills/Trusts	_____	_____	_____
Deed to property	_____	_____	_____
Life insurance policies	_____	_____	_____
Birth certificate	_____	_____	_____
Stock/bond certificates	_____	_____	_____
Investment papers (such as limited partnership certificates)	_____	_____	_____
Auto Registration (Pink Slip)	_____	_____	_____
IRA paperwork	_____	_____	_____
Business Agreements	_____	_____	_____
Company retirement benefits	_____	_____	_____
Other (list)			
_____	_____	_____	_____
_____	_____	_____	_____

The executor/executrix of your will should have a copy of this information in order to help facilitate the settlement of your estate.

(This page may be reproduced without further permission)

APPENDIX B

COMPOUND INTEREST TABLES

ONE DOLLAR LEFT ON DEPOSIT

Year	6%	8%	10%	12%	15%
1	1.06	1.08	1.10	1.12	1.15
2	1.12	1.17	1.21	1.25	1.32
3	1.19	1.26	1.33	1.40	1.52
4	1.26	1.36	1.46	1.57	1.75
5	1.34	1.47	1.61	1.76	2.01
6	1.42	1.59	1.77	1.97	2.31
7	1.50	1.71	1.95	2.21	2.66
8	1.59	1.85	2.14	2.48	3.06
9	1.69	1.99	2.36	2.77	3.52
10	1.79	2.16	2.59	3.10	4.05
11	1.90	2.33	2.85	3.48	4.65
12	2.01	2.52	3.14	3.90	5.35
13	2.13	2.72	3.45	4.36	6.15
14	2.26	2.94	3.80	4.89	7.08
15	2.40	3.17	4.18	5.47	8.14
16	2.54	3.43	4.60	6.13	9.36
17	2.69	3.70	5.05	6.87	10.76
18	2.85	4.00	5.56	7.69	12.38
19	3.03	4.32	6.12	8.61	14.23
20	3.21	4.66	6.73	9.65	16.37
25	4.29	6.85	10.83	17.00	32.92
30	5.74	10.06	17.45	29.96	66.22

EXAMPLE: One dollar left on deposit for 10 years at 8% will grow to $2.16.

Go down the year column to the 10th year. Then come over to the 8% column to get the figure of 2.16. Then $1.00 × 2.16 = $2.16.

APPENDIX B

COMPOUND INTEREST TABLE

ONE DOLLAR DEPOSITED AT THE END OF EACH YEAR				
6%	8%	10%	12%	15%

Year	6%	8%	10%	12%	15%
1	1.00	1.00	1.00	1.00	1.00
2	2.06	2.08	2.10	2.12	2.15
3	3.18	3.25	3.31	3.37	3.47
4	4.37	4.51	4.64	4.78	4.99
5	5.64	5.87	6.11	6.35	6.74
6	6.98	7.34	7.72	8.12	8.75
7	8.39	8.92	9.49	10.09	11.07
8	9.90	10.64	11.44	12.30	13.73
9	11.49	12.49	13.58	14.78	16.79
10	13.18	14.49	15.94	17.55	20.30
11	14.97	16.65	18.53	20.65	24.35
12	16.87	18.98	21.38	24.13	29.00
13	18.88	21.50	24.52	28.03	34.35
14	21.02	24.21	27.98	32.39	40.50
15	23.28	27.15	31.77	37.28	47.58
16	25.67	30.32	35.95	42.75	55.72
17	28.21	33.75	40.54	48.88	65.08
18	30.91	37.45	45.60	55.75	75.84
19	33.76	41.45	51.16	63.44	88.21
20	36.79	45.76	57.27	72.05	102.44
25	54.86	73.11	98.35	133.33	212.79
30	79.06	113.28	164.49	241.33	434.75

ONE DOLLAR DEPOSITED EACH YEAR

EXAMPLE: One dollar deposited at the end of each year for 15 years earning 10% will grow to a total of $31.77.

Go down the year column to the 15th year. Then come over to the 10% column to get the figure of 31.77. Then $1.00 × 31.77 = $31.77.

APPENDIX C

RESOURCE INFORMATION FOR RETIREES

Protect yourself and your family from future financial hardship by educating yourself now. Learn as much as you can about your retirement years. Write to the resources below to get more information.

Consumer Information Center
Pueblo, CO 81009
  For catalog of free and low-cost government publications.

American Association of Retired Persons
1090 ''K'' Street, NW
Washington, DC 20044
  Private organization that provides help and support for retirees.

Social Security Administration
6401 Security Boulevard
Baltimore, MD 21235
  To receive a free statement of earnings credited to your Social Security record, call your nearest Social Security office for more information.

Administration on Aging
c/o Department of Health and Human Services
200 Independence Avenue, SW
Washington, DC 20201
  Free booklets on services for the elderly.

Veterans Administration
810 Vermont Avenue, NW
Washington, DC 20201
  Provides a variety of services for qualified veterans.

APPENDIX D

THE INDIVIDUAL RETIREMENT ACCOUNT (IRA)

Every wage earner will still be able to put money into an IRA (the limit is $2,000 a year* or 100% of compensation, whichever is less), but many people will no longer be able to claim an IRA deduction on their future tax returns.

Whether you can claim an IRA deduction or not depends on your level of income and whether you are an active participant in a retirement plan at work. In either case, the funds in your IRA will compound tax free until withdrawn.

Individuals still eligible for a full IRA tax deduction include:

- single individuals not covered by an employer sponsored retirement plan

- single individuals whose adjusted gross income (AGI) before the IRA deduction is less than $25,000

- married couples whose AGI is less than $40,000 (regardless of whether or not either is covered by a company retirement plan)

- married couples in which neither spouse is in a company retirement plan regardless of total income

In addition, a partial IRA tax deduction is still possible in cases where:

- one or both married partners are participants in an employer sponsored retirement plan and have an AGI of $40,000 or over but less than $50,000

- a single individual who is a participant in a company sponsored retirement plan and has an AGI of $25,000 or over but less than $35,000.

---

*A married individual with a non-working spouse may contribute a total of $2,250.

REVIEWERS

The publisher would like to acknowledge the several individuals who reviewed various drafts of this material and thank them for their suggestions and contributions. Our special thanks to:

Charles Atwell, Kansas City, Missouri

Elwood N. Chapman, Seal Beach, California

Michael Feder, Foster City, California

Daniel Gray, Menlo Park, California

Noel Johnson, Orlando, Florida

Mitchell F. Keil, Fountain Valley, California

Edward I. McQuiston, Palo Alto, California

Gloria Mitchell, Cupertino, California

Mary Kay Voss, Bellevue, Washington

Judy Watt, Redondo Beach, California

124

NOTES

FOR OTHER FIFTY-MINUTE SELF-STUDY BOOKS
SEE THE BACK OF THIS BOOK.

NOTES

FOR OTHER FIFTY-MINUTE SELF-STUDY BOOKS
SEE THE BACK OF THIS BOOK.

SPECIAL ORDER FORM

Crisp Publications, Inc. publishes several books that are appropriate for retirement planning programs. These fine books may be ordered directly using the following form.

TO: CRISP PUBLICATIONS, INC.
95 FIRST STREET
LOS ALTOS, CA 94022

☐ YES, I would like to order at no risk* the following CPI books at prices shown, plus shipping and billing.**

Quantity	*Title*		*Amount*
_____	COMFORT ZONES: A PRACTICAL GUIDE FOR RETIREMENT PLANNING 2/C (Book Format) (320 pages)	$13.95	_____
_____	COMFORT ZONES: A PRACTICAL GUIDE FOR RETIREMENT PLANNING 2/C (Loose-Leaf Edition) (300 pages)	$14.95	_____
_____	COMFORT ZONES: LEADER'S GUIDE 2/C (Binder) (156 pages)	$29.95	_____
_____	INVENTORY OF RETIREMENT ACTIVITIES (16 pages — Inventory)	$ 1.95	_____
_____	THE COMPLETE & EASY GUIDE TO SOCIAL SECURITY & MEDICARE (Annual Edition) (200 pages)	$11.95	_____
_____	THE UNFINISHED BUSINESS OF LIVING: YOU AND YOUR AGING PARENTS (250 pages)	$12.95	_____
_____	FINANCIAL PLANNING WITH EMPLOYEE BENEFITS	$ 7.95	_____

Postage and handling** _____
California Tax _____
TOTAL AMOUNT _____
ENCLOSED

Ship To: _____
_____
_____

Bill To: (Billing available only on company purchase order #'s)
_____
_____
_____
_____

☐ Send Volume Purchase Discount Information

*No Risk: If for <u>any</u> reason, I am not completely satisfied, I understand the materials may be returned within 30 days for a full refund.

**$1.50 for first book, $.50 for each book thereafter.

ABOUT THE FIFTY-MINUTE SERIES

We hope you enjoyed this book and found it valuable. If so, we have good news for you. This title is part of the best selling *FIFTY-MINUTE Series* of books. All other books are similar in size and identical in price. Several books are supported with a training video. These are identified by the symbol **V** next to the title.

Since the first *FIFTY-MINUTE* book appeared in 1986, more than five million copies have been sold worldwide. Each book was developed with the reader in mind. The result is a concise, high quality module written in a positive, readable self-study format.

FIFTY-MINUTE Books and Videos are available from your distributor or from Crisp Publications, Inc., 95 First Street, Los Altos, CA 94022. A free current catalog is available on request.

The complete list of *FIFTY-MINUTE Series* Books and Videos are listed on the following pages and organized by general subject area.

MANAGEMENT TRAINING (Cont.)

PERSONNEL/HUMAN RESOURCES

COMMUNICATIONS

CUSTOMER SERVICE/SALES TRAINING (CONT.)

SMALL BUSINESS/FINANCIAL PLANNING

ADULT LITERACY/BASIC LEARNING

CAREER BUILDING

To order books/videos from the FIFTY-MINUTE Series, please:

1. **CONTACT YOUR DISTRIBUTOR**

   or

2. **Write to Crisp Publications, Inc.**
   95 First Street   (415) 949-4888 - phone
   Los Altos, CA 94022   (415) 949-1610 - FAX